The Cistercians

Piedra, Spain. Nave, *Cul-de-lampe*, or corbel

The Cistercians

Monks and Monasteries
of Europe

Stephen Tobin

The Herbert Press

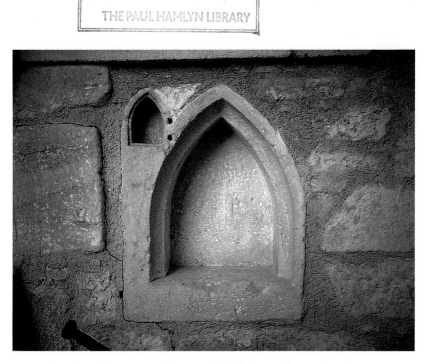

FRONTISPIECE Maulbronn, Germany. Wash house, fountain

ABOVE Bebenhausen, Germany. Niche by stair descending through curtain wall. The larger niche held a lantern, while the smaller held tinder and flint. Both have lost their doors

First published in Great Britain 1995 by
The Herbert Press Ltd,
46 Northchurch Road, London N1 4EJ
House editor: Susan Malvern
Designed by: Pauline Harrison
Set in Centaur
Typeset by Nene Phototypesetters Ltd,
Northampton
Printed and bound in Hong Kong by
South China Printing Co. (1988) Ltd

A CIP catalogue record for this book is available from the British Library.

ISBN 1 871569 80 X

Contents

Acknowledgements

My first debt must be to those owners or custodians of abbeys and former abbeys who so kindly allowed me to visit and photograph their properties:

M. Mauvais of Reigny, General and Mme du Pontavice of Le Reclus (who met my request to take a few shots of the abbey with the remark: 'If you wish to visit our house then you shall do so properly or not at all!' and promptly gave me a full guided tour); Signor Tanini of the Badia a Settimo; the owners of Mariental, Rosières, Jouy, La Ferté, La Charmoye, Ecurey (where I was shown not only the twelfth-century lay brothers' refectory but also, quite unexpectedly, a unique private collection of nineteenth and twentieth century European and American tractors not usually open to the public), Froidmont, Quincy, L'Isle-en-Barrois, Lanvaux, Boulancourt, Larrivour, Escarp, Biddlesden, Garendon, Coggeshall, Merevale, Stoneleigh, Robertsbridge (where a kitchen garden now covers the site of the chapterhouse. When I explained this to the owner, she exclaimed: 'What? You mean to tell me there are abbots buried under my cabbages!'), Boxley, Sant'Agostino di Montalto and La Matina.

M. Lebrun of Vaucelles and Bob the warden of Thame (both of whom gave me personal guided tours of the properties in their care), the charming Eva of Zlata Koruna, the residents of the village of Sagittario, and the custodians of Bonport, Prières, Cercamp, Vignogoul, Landais, Valle Crucis and Vale Royal.

The nuns of Llantarnam, Acquafredda, La Trinità di Cortona, Boquen, La Maigrauge and Gradefes; Dom Gabriel of Stams and the monks of La Trappe, Aiguebelle, Wilhering, Schlierbach (where father prior gave me an exhaustive tour of the abbey and then pressed two cheeses from the monks' own farm on me for my picnic); Le Tre Fontane, Galeso, Hauterive and Huerta (where we were offered yet more cheese); the parish priest of Fitero (who kindly waived the rule that all photography requires the permission of the Bishop of Pamplona); the incumbents of Sambucina,

Arabona, S. Maria in Strada, Buonsollazzo and San Martino al Cimino, and the vicar of Abbey Dore.

My especial thanks must also go to the warder in charge of France's top security prison, the former abbey of Clairvaux, who kindly allowed me to view (though understandably not to photograph) the magnificent remains of the lay brothers' building dating back to the time of St Bernard; also to the firemen stationed in the erstwhile refectory of the Collège des Bernardins in Paris who let me visit and photograph their 'barracks'.

On a more personal level, I shall not forget the kindness and interest shown by Hélène Palouzie of the Caisse Nationale des Monuments Historiques et des Sites in Montpellier, who shared with me both her immense knowledge of the Languedoc and her generous hospitality. Dom Goffredo Viti oc of the Certosa in Florence not only made numerous valuable suggestions but also gave me the freedom of the monastery's well-stocked library. Gerry Slowey of the University of Birmingham kindly sent me much useful information. My thanks must also go to my wife Blandine, my daughter Héloïse and my family and friends for their support and interest, and the patience many of them have shown while trekking across half of Europe in search of Cistercian abbeys, in conditions ranging from blinding snowstorms in North Yorkshire to the sweltering heat of Apulia in summer, from the thick mud of rain-drenched Brittany to the unforgiving dust of the Castilian meseta, often to find that only a few stones (if that) were left.

My last mention can only be for Maurizio Bossi of the Gabinetto Vieusseux in Florence, who alone must shoulder the responsibility for the conception of this book. It was he who, as we sat in a trattoria in deepest Abruzzo enjoying the spit-roast lamb and Montepulciano, cried out in despair: 'After this lunch, I refuse to set foot in any more Cistercian abbeys, unless you start doing something useful with all those slides you take – like writing a book, or something …'.

I make no attempt to hide my enormous debt to the scholarship of Dom Louis Lekai oc of the University of Dallas, but it goes without saying that any errors, omissions, hypotheses or conclusions in this book are my own.

Having visited over 300 Cistercian sites, I find it encouraging to record that I have been well received at all but six.

OVERLEAF Fossanova, Italy. Nave

Introduction

FOUNTAINS ABBEY, in North Yorkshire, attracts more visitors in a year than any other monument in England except the Tower of London. The Abbey of Las Huelgas, outside Burgos, is visited by more people daily than the city's cathedral, one of the glories of Spanish Gothic architecture. The Abbey of Fontenay, in Burgundy, is one of the few monuments in France to have been accorded the status of World Heritage Site by UNESCO. When it was decided to make a film of Umberto Eco's best-selling novel *The Name of the Rose*, a story about a Franciscan sleuth set in a Benedictine monastery, the film makers had no hesitation in choosing the Abbey of Eberbach, on the Rhine, as the perfect location. The Italian radio programme for lorry drivers, 'Mondo Camion', strongly urged its listeners to visit the Abbeys of Fossanova and Casamari as soon as they could afford to take a little time off work for sightseeing, describing the two abbeys as oases of calm after the stress of driving a juggernaut for long hours on the motorway. These six abbeys have two things in common: they all manifestly exercise some form of magnetic attraction on a considerable proportion of the European public 'at leisure', and they are all Cistercian.

Professor Braunfels, in his classic work *Monasteries of Western Europe*, chooses an illustration of the cloister of Fontenay as his frontispiece, and opens Chapter 1 with these words: 'Whoever sets foot in some peaceful haven of the Cistercians, whoever comes upon a scene of ruins in the snow, a church choir forgotten in the woods, … is moved by them. Solemnity, calm and dignity speak from these stones'. At many Cistercian sites today, the little kiosk where you buy your ticket, not unlike a cinema box-office, and the waste-paper baskets and well-meaning signposts or, where the ruins have not been taken into care, the cars parked right up against the crumbling walls and all the trappings of Sunday outings, from the remains of picnics to candy-floss stalls, do little to sustain the feeling of awe described by Braunfels. And yet despite all this, these ruins still have the power to move even the most jaded contemporary sensibilities.

OPPOSITE Buildwas, England. Nave

Why? Is a ruin anything but a worthless pile of old stones? Certainly up until the French Revolution anyone suggesting that it was would have been taken for an eccentric. At best, ruins were a handy source of ready-cut building material simply asking to be reused. If we appreciate the beauty and understand the scientific and archeological importance of ruins today, we owe this almost wholly to the Romantic movement, which began in England in the late eighteenth century. As with the enthusiasm for nature, it grew out of a common European preoccupation. A feeling of uneasiness, which was a direct result of the political turmoil surrounding the French Revolution, created a new sympathy for the Middle Ages. In the eyes of the Romantics, beauty was no longer automatically associated with classical perfection. The emotion a work of art excited had taken the place of the objective criterion of flawless form. The imagination of the perceiver became at least as important as the technical mastery of the artist, and it was not long before that imagination turned its attention to the ivy-covered ruins of castle and abbey. In truth, the Romantics had been preceded almost two centuries earlier by the English playwright John Webster, whose Antonio, in the Duchess of Malfi, exclaims:

> I do love these ancient ruins.
> We never tread upon them but we set
> Our foot upon some reverend history:
> And, questionless, here in this open court,
> Which now lies naked to the injuries
> Of stormy weather, some men lie interr'd
> Lov'd the church so well, and gave so largely to 't,
> They thought it should have canopied their bones
> Till doomsday ...

A century later, the Buck brothers were making sketches of many of the finest abbey ruins in England and Wales, while John Aubrey described the remains of the Cistercian Abbey of Waverley in these words:

> The Abby is situated, though low, in a very good Air, and is as Romantick a Place as most I have seen. Here is a fine Rivulet runs under the House and fences one Side ... Here also remain Walls of a fair Church ... and within the Quadrangle of the Cloysters was a Pond, but now is a Marsh.

But these still uncommon views were not to acquire any degree of currency for another hundred years. By the late 1700s, the 'Romantick' quality of ruins had become fashionable, but their scientific value was unrecognized and no attempt was made to preserve them as historical relics. When the owners of the Yorkshire abbeys of Roche and Fountains decided to improve the 'Romantick' aspect of their ruins, they felt no compunction at using the weapon of demolition to achieve the picturesque effect they were seeking. It was only in the early years of the nineteenth century that the prevailing romantic mood encouraged the scholarly study of medieval architecture. Rudimentary archeological excavation began to be undertaken, and even the landscaping of privately owned ruins betrayed a more scientific approach. When the ruins of another Yorkshire abbey, Jervaulx, were incorporated into a landscaped park in the early 1800s, the tables were turned and it was the ruins which influenced the layout of the garden rather than vice versa.

The Industrial Revolution and the psychological alienation it created among the newly urbanized classes, was instrumental in reviving interest in the Middle Ages; the calm of the cloister was seen as a haven of peace by those who could no longer bear the nerve-racking drumming of the cotton mills and the filthy smoke belching from factory chimneys. Considered 'barbaric' ever since the sixteenth century, the Middle Ages were now seen as a mythical golden 'age of faith', in contrast to the degenerate atheism and materialism of modern times. The severity of Puritanism and the rationality of the Enlightenment were replaced by a sentimental longing for the pageantry and colour of medieval religion, and neo-Gothic architecture was to be its vehicle. Post-Reformation furnishings were ruthlessly ripped out of surviving medieval churches, which were equally as ruthlessly 'restored' to their original appearance. In this climate, the appeal of ruined Gothic abbeys was assured. The example of Kirkstall, in Yorkshire, is typical. When the abbey was painted by William Richardson in the 1840s, it was in the middle of the countryside. Rapid urban expansion soon brought it within easy distance of Leeds, one of the most important centres of the industrial revolution in the country. The City Council acquired the site in 1889 and turned the grounds into a public park for the material and spiritual recreation of the urban population.

In the rest of Europe the nineteenth century was still very much a time of wanton demolition, which the heartfelt but isolated pleas of enlightened public functionaries such as Prosper Mérimée and Viollet-le-Duc in

France, or the influence of artistic groups such as the Nazarenes and their quasi-monastic 'Guild of St Luke' in Germany and northern Europe, were by and large unable to stop. The early years of this century, however, saw the spread of the appreciation of monastic ruins and, by extension, of surviving monastic architecture, from England to the Continent. The Abbey of Fontenay, spared after the Revolution through being turned into a paper factory by Élie de Montgolfier, was restored to its original purity of form by his descendant Edouard Aynard in 1911. Noirlac, a porcelain factory until 1894, was bought by the Département du Cher in 1909, although restoration work only got under way in 1950. Les Vaux-de-Cernay was bought in the nineteenth century by the de Rothschild family and turned into a country retreat. In this century it has become a luxury hotel. The former abbey of San Pietro alla Canonica, in Amalfi, was already a 'romantic' hotel at the end of the last century, while the same fate overtook Piedra, in Castile, in the early years of this century. Eberbach was used as a prison after its secularization in 1813, and remained so until restoration work began in 1926. Valserena, the abbey which inspired Stendhal to write his *La Chartreuse de Parme*, was a tomato purée factory until the outbreak of World War II: restoration is still in progress. As late as the 1950s, the Abbey of Clairmont, in Maine, was scheduled for demolition by the authorities in charge of France's artistic heritage. Luckily the sensitivity of the explosives expert sent to blow the church up prevented him from placing his charges. Since the blinkered destruction of so much 'uncouth' and 'socially useless' medieval architecture after the Revolution, the wheel had turned full circle, and two sisters, who had fallen in love with the ruins, purchased Clairmont and restored it for no other reason than to offer it for public enjoyment and edification. The Romantic ethic, supported by the standing which the discipline of archeology now enjoyed in scientific circles, had triumphed. Where previous centuries saw ruins as a simple pile of stones which it was a shame not to exploit, we, who have inherited the Romantic movement's understanding of 'atmosphere', cannot but respond to the call of the whispering walls and 'bare ruin'd choirs'. Indeed the current tendency among archeologists is to encourage ruins to keep their 'romantic' unkempt look, after their counterparts in the early part of this century, headed by Sir Charles Peers, the Chief Inspector of Ancient Monuments in Britain, had popularized the now common 'didactic' appearance of closely-mown lawns and vacuumed masonry.

The battle to preserve abbey ruins and monastic architecture from the philistine attacks of the insensitive clearly involves the buildings of all orders. But what is special about the Cistercians that their abbeys should attract so many more visitors than those of any other order? The very fact that the Cistercians contrived to build their monasteries 'far from the commerce of men', in what were wild and impossibly isolated valley floors in the twelfth century and are now, for the most part, charming out-of-the-way rural settings, is undoubtedly a major factor. The setting of a Cistercian abbey is almost invariably one of great beauty, thanks partly to the skills in husbandry of the monks, who 'tamed' their chosen wildernesses, and partly to a growing awareness and appreciation in Europe today of our natural environment. The ubiquitous presence of flowing water is another key to the secret of Cistercian sites, and this is no accident. In the Middle Ages it was said that 'while Benedict built on the mountain top, Bernard chose the valley'; not only was running water essential to the material needs of the monastery, but springs and rivers have always been imbued with magical powers since the dawn of mankind, and in the Christian tradition they were dedicated to the Virgin. St Bernard of Clairvaux, the driving force behind Cistercian expansion in the twelfth century, had a special devotion to the Mother of God and insisted that all abbey churches were dedicated to her.

Another bewitching quality to be found in Cistercian abbeys lies in the breathtaking beauty and simplicity of the architecture. Born in rebellion against the gaudy exuberance of contemporary Romanesque, Cistercian architecture is a byword for clarity, precision and simplicity. The modern predilection for bare stonework, which can be traced back to the sensibility of aesthetes such as John Ruskin, had never existed before the last century — with one exception: the Cistercians. In their own day the Cistercians, with their bare, hull-like churches, were an eccentricity in the colourful panorama of contemporary architecture. Today the functionality of their design appeals instantly to the modern predilection for understated harmony.

Finally, the nationalism which characterized Europe from the Renaissance to the end of World War II is being rapidly replaced by a new sense of belonging on two levels, the European and the regional, which are complementary rather than contradictory. Hand in hand with an increasing awareness, made possible by the advent of mass tourism, of a cultural heritage with undeniable common roots going back to the

San Martino al Cimino, Italy. The abstract elegance of this lotus-flower capital well illustrates the skill of the local stonecutters in conjugating their artistry with the Order's ban on the anthropomorphic and grotesque carving typical of contemporary Romanesque sculpture classical world and beyond, there is a new need to safeguard regional identity against the risk of bland uniformity.

One of the major factors in forming our common European heritage was the Christian religion. Whether we subscribe to its teachings today or not, we are likely to think of 'cultural tourism' in whatever part of Europe as involving a visit to a handful of 'old churches'. And once inside, certain things like a crucifix, a baptismal font or a pulpit are reassuringly familiar. After the fall of the Roman Empire, the Church remained the greatest patron of the arts in Europe until the beginning of this century. While the idea of modern architecture is likely to conjure up an office block or some other utilitarian structure, if we think of Romanesque or Gothic architecture, we will almost certainly think of a church, and whether we are in Scotland, Sicily or Spain we will instantly recognize the two styles. Yet the light and scintillating Sicilian Romanesque, influenced by local Arab tradition, is a totally different style to the heavy Norman architecture of the British Isles, and the Cathedral of Florence, while undeniably Gothic, could never be mistaken for Chartres or Amiens. What we have, in effect, is a series of uniquely regional interpretations of style resting on a common base, and this brings us back to our initial premise. The exploration of ecclesiastical architecture is a rewarding experience which inevitably leads to increased awareness of our common European heritage, made up of a fascinating kaleidoscope of regional and local variations on a number of stylistic themes.

The Cistercian Order, within this framework, occupies a unique position. One of the last great pan-European phenomena before the triumph of the nation-state, the order acknowledged, and was politically able in twelfth-century Europe to acknowledge, no other sovereign than the Pope. When the founding fathers of Cîteaux instituted the first real monastic family, where every abbey down the family tree owed its ultimate allegiance to the mother-house in Burgundy, they did so without it even crossing their minds that this allegiance might one day be seen as dangerous. By the time of the Hundred Years War, for instance, in the fourteenth century, many Cistercian houses in England were considered potential hotbeds of treachery, owing obedience as they did to a mother-house in France, and transferring monies to it on a regular basis. That this suspicion was not unfounded is borne out by comparison with what had happened in Germany two centuries before. When Frederick Barbarossa, the Holy Roman Emperor, insisted upon the recognition of

Byland, England. West front

OPPOSITE Las Huelgas, Spain. 'Small' cloister. St Bernard thundered against the fantastic bestiaries and grotesque gargoyles which populated the capitals of Cluniac cloisters, distracting monks and nuns from their meditation on things spiritual. As this striking detail shows, plain geometric patterns and stylized foliage were not the only substitute for such 'abominations'. This miniature church façade was designed to direct the thoughts of the sisters towards the heavenly Jerusalem

an antipope, the German Cluniacs followed his instructions, while the German Cistercians followed the lead of their Order as a whole and refused to obey him, their temporal overlord. For the Cistercians, man's prior obligation was to God, and theirs in particular was to God via the abbot of their mother-house. They considered themselves exempt from allegiance to any temporal master, and were granted real exemption by the Papacy from obedience to their immediate spiritual lord, the local bishop. An abbey was known as *abbatia nullius*, an abbey belonging to no one, since it belonged to the Order alone and owed allegiance to no one but the Pope. It is hardly surprising to find the Cistercians espousing the cause of, and indeed harbouring, Thomas Becket in his quarrel with King Henry II over the right of felons in holy orders to be tried by the church rather than by the state. Nor is it surprising to find them mediating in affairs of such importance for the Continent as a whole as the Cathar heresy, the crusades, or the countless quarrels between the emerging power of the national monarchies and the old trans-European institutions of Papacy and Empire, or at times between the princes of Christendom themselves. While the history of the Order after the golden age of the twelfth and thirteenth centuries, with the creation of national congregations and so forth, is very much one of adaptation to the requirements of a continent divided into nations, the vision of the founders embraced the whole of Europe, or Christendom as they would have called it, without distinction.

The art and architecture of the Cistercians reflect the Order's adherence to this unwritten principle with remarkable constancy. In an age where design was transmitted by direct contact, word of mouth and the roughest of drawings, the Cistercians 'exported' their interpretation of the plainest twelfth-century Burgundian architecture to the four corners of Europe, reproducing wherever they went, and with astonishing accuracy, the earthly Jerusalem which they identified with their mother-house. And yet, as Christopher Holdsworth points out, 'if ... one looks at the [statutes] as a whole, from the beginnings to the late thirteenth century, one cannot fail to be struck by what is not covered. There is ... not a word about the size and shape of any of the buildings ... in 1192 the chapter could condemn a dormitory as having been built contrary to the form and customs of the order in the expectation that everyone would know what was meant.' Yet nowhere can we find a prescription for the ideal dormitory, or indeed for any new building, in Cistercian documents. But armed with a ground plan of a standard Cistercian monastery (see page 21), the

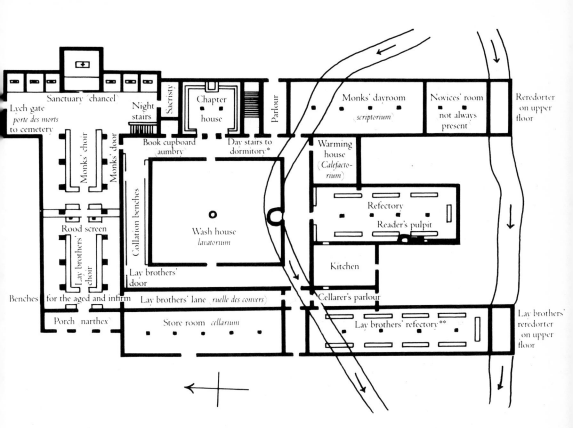

Sanctuary chancel

Lych gate
porte des morts
to cemetery

Monks' choir

Monks' door

Night stairs

Sacristy

Chapter house

Parlour

Monks' dayroom
scriptorium

Novices' room
not always present

Reredorter
on upper
floor

Book cupboard
aumbry

Day stairs to
dormitory*

Warming
house
(*Calefacto-
rium*)

Rood screen

Collation benches

Wash house
lavatorium

Refectory

Reader's pulpit

Lay brothers' choir

Lay brothers' door

Kitchen

Benches for the aged and infirm

Lay brothers' lane *ruelle des convers*

Cellarer's parlour

Porch narthex

Store room *cellarium*

Lay brothers' refectory**

Lay brothers'
reredorter
on upper
floor

* The monks' dormitory lay over the entire east range   ** The lay-brothers' dormitory lay over the entire west range

Plan of a typical Cistercian abbey

modern visitor has absolutely no trouble in locating the whereabouts of the individual buildings or rooms, whether he be in Denmark, Portugal or Sardinia. And yet twelfth-century uniformity of spirit was a far cry from the standardization of today. The same visitor, while deriving a warm sense of satisfaction from the familiarity of his surroundings, is likely to be intrigued and fascinated by the concessions to local tradition evident in the buildings around him. The creative tension engendered by the conflict between the aspirations of local stonemasons and sculptors, and the stringent precepts of the Order's artistic policies, is responsible for some of the most appealing architecture in Europe, architecture that is at once immediately recognizable and richly articulated, satisfying the visitor's need to conjugate the familiar with the novel.

Fontaine-Guérard, France. The siting of this nunnery is perfectly 'Cistercian', a narrow valley by the source of a stream

Fontaine-Guérard, France. Nave. Most nunneries had aisleless naves

1. The Foundation in the Desert

THE CISTERCIANS first appeared on the scene of medieval Burgundy towards the end of the eleventh century, in an age where national boundaries had yet to make an impression on the collective consciousness.

Until that time, western monasticism had relied almost entirely on the rule of Benedict of Nursia to give it form and structure, yet Benedict himself (*c.* AD 480–550) would have been the first to express surprise at the idea of his rule spawning an 'Order'. It was in fact only under Pope Leo XIII in the late 1800s that the followers of his rule were pulled together into a single congregation, and to this day the independence of Benedictine houses is jealously guarded. The Abbot Primate of the Order is in effect no more than a figurehead.

Benedict was inspired by a rich tradition of monasticism transmitted from the Middle East to the West through many channels, possibly including the writings of a fourth-century monk called John Cassian. What Benedict had done, in the simplest terms, was to suggest to those who wished to renounce the world and give their life to God, and to do so by living in a community rather than in or before moving on to a hermitage, that it would be for the best if there were an abbot (from the Aramaic 'abbas' or 'father') to govern that community, giving it the spiritual benefit of his wisdom and experience and keeping a fatherly eye on the orderly running of its daily life.

It was by historical circumstance rather than by design that the structure of the Roman *domus* (house) to which the followers of Benedict were accustomed, with its functional rooms and offices arranged around an enclosed inner atrium (sheltered courtyard), was adapted to form the classic monastery laid out around a cloister. Just as it had been the domain of the 'cloistered' womenfolk in imperial times, so it lent itself admirably to the needs of an enclosed self-supporting community in barbarian sixth-century Italy.

Benedict propounded, in his 'little rule for beginners', a life of severity and humility, balanced by a healthy dose of humanity and sound practical good sense. Total obedience to the abbot was tempered by the obligation laid on the abbot himself to take counsel of the whole community. The monk's day was to be divided between work about the monastery and what Benedict called 'God's work' (*opus Dei*, literally 'God's work' – totally unrelated to the modern Catholic institution of the same name). Monastic work included gardening and household chores, although the practice of agriculture on the scale it took in the later Middle Ages seems not to have formed any part of Benedict's thinking. God's work combined moments of private prayer and meditation with community worship in the oratory – more akin to a simple house of prayer than to our idea of a monumental abbey church.

The concentrated power of any ideal which gains common currency tends to become more and more diluted as it spreads. Benedict's rule was no exception. By the end of the tenth century, when his rule had been accepted in almost every monastery in Christendom, it was ripe for reform.

Two distinct trends in monastic reform can be distinguished during this period: the first is almost wholly an Italian phenomenon, while the second is essentially Burgundian. Italy during this period was the seat of the Papacy and as such was unavoidably at the centre of the cut-and-thrust power politics of the day. The Pope was becoming increasingly aware of his temporal 'responsibilities', which opposed him sometimes bitterly to the ambitions of the Holy Roman Emperor, and distracted him and his entire curia from what should have been the spiritual concerns of his mission.

This involvement of the Church in temporal quarrels and worldly affairs provoked a reaction in the more spiritually sensitive men of the day. Thus it is no accident that three of the greatest reformers came from central Italy, the Pope's own hunting ground.

St Romuald fled to the secluded valley of the Casentino, in Tuscany, where he founded the abbey of Camaldoli. In a literal attempt to interpret the rule of St Benedict, he built a monastery for beginners at the bottom of the slope and a series of individual hermitages for more seasoned ascetics on top of the mountain overlooking the valley. St Giovanni Gualberto took to the hills around Florence, founding an isolated monastery deep in the forest of Vallombrosa where the echoes of political

Follina, Italy. Cloister, east walk, showing typical decoration: plaster painted to resemble the poor materials it conceals

OPPOSITE Tintern, Wales. The ruins of Tintern Abbey, in the solitary Wye Valley, were among the first to capture the imagination of the eighteenth-century Romantics

turmoil could not penetrate. Peter Damian's retreat from the world was a hermitage high in the Appennines on the borders of Umbria and the Marches, at Fonte Avellana, where he spent his life writing and in meditation, as far removed from the troubles of his time as possible.

The second strain which we can discern in the movement towards monastic reform was not so much a return to the spirit and letter of Benedict's original rule as a move towards adapting the monastic phenomenon to contemporary political conditions – a far more worldly enterprise altogether. In AD 909, the Duke of Aquitaine had bequeathed some land he owned in Burgundy for the foundation of a Benedictine monastery that should acknowledge no authority other than the Pope's. Given the weakness of the Papacy in the tenth and eleventh centuries, however, it quickly became clear that it was the Pope who would be leaning on the monks for support and protection rather than the other way around.

That Cluny, as the new foundation was known, was able in the course of two hundred years to exercise immense political influence and in so doing to accrue the great wealth it did, was due in part to a succession of hard-headed and extremely able abbots and in part to its geographical position. Cluny was situated in an area which was at the time under the suzerainty of neither the Emperor nor the King of France. The abbey was thus at liberty to put into practice its proclaimed allegiance to the Pope, and to advertise this fact by dedicating the churches of all its foundations to St Peter.

While Cluny founded many abbeys and priories, it never really organized them into any form of structured family, simply concentrating all power over them into its own hands. The two salient features of Cluniac monasticism, apart from involvement in temporal affairs, concern the movement's approach to liturgy and the plastic arts.

A Cluniac monk dedicated the greater part of his day to the celebration of church services, to the almost total neglect not only of manual labour but even of private prayer and study. A monk from Cluny by the name of Ulrich, in 1075, wrote a full account of life there, and readily confesses that the greater part of the day, and night, was taken up in fulfilling liturgical obligations in church, such as the singing of hymns, psalms and litanies, including at times the whole Psalter, interspersed with readings from the Bible and the church fathers. Not surprisingly, there was very little time left to do anything else.

Under the man whom some consider the greatest of Cluny's abbot-potentates, Peter the Venerable, Cluny in the early twelfth century witnessed a flowering of Romanesque art the like of which had rarely been seen before. In keeping with the Cluniac theory that no cost should be spared in adorning the house of God, the Abbey Church at Cluny (destroyed during the French Revolution) was ablaze with brilliant colours, its capitals alive with a writhing bestiary, its floors a carpet of brightly coloured tiles and its furnishings a treasure chest of gold and silver, enamel and precious stones. While the church and cloister at Cluny have both gone, one can get an idea of how richly the abbey must have been decorated by looking at the cloister of Moissac, the church of the Madeleine at Vézelay, or the treasure of Ste Foy at Conques.

And yet for all the arrogant attachment to worldly power and soft if not luxurious living usually associated with Cluny, the impression we are left with after reading the letters of Peter the Venerable is one of great warmth and humanity. While the language Peter uses is invariably flowery and in many ways excessive, resembling the sculpture and frescoes he encouraged in his church and cloisters, his writings are permeated with a spirit of charity and compassion for human frailty. He approved of hermitage, but understood that not everybody could aspire to such perfection. He was an orthodox theologian, one of the most eminent of his time, yet it was at Cluny under Peter's fatherly eye that Peter Abelard found refuge after his final defeat and humiliation. He was an unswerving upholder of the Papacy, yet commissioned the first translation into Latin of the Qu'ran.

In a religious climate which encompassed both the burning single-minded fervour of Saints Romuald and Giovanni Gualberto and the all-embracing generosity of spirit of Peter the Venerable, it is perhaps not surprising to find a number of Cluniac monks who felt that the life they were leading was rather less in keeping with the spirit of St Benedict's rule than they would have liked. Indeed St Romuald himself had started his monastic career as a Cluniac. But he lived in Italy where the worldly preoccupations of the clergy drove him to seek the peace and solitude of a virtual hermitage in order to find his path back to God. In France, discontent with the monastic world arose from within that world itself.

In 1098, a group of monks seeking to perfect their way of life in stricter observance of the rule of St Benedict, abandoned the Cluniac abbey of Molesme in Burgundy and followed their Abbot Robert to found a new monastery. It is worth pausing for a while to examine briefly the career of Abbot Robert before 1098.

Bénisson-Dieu, France. Early Cistercian nave, fifteenth-century roof

OPPOSITE Caugé, France. Barn: a grange of the Abbey of La Noé

Born around 1028 in Champagne, Robert joined the monastery of Montier-la-Celle, near Troyes, very early in life, and at the age of about twenty-six was already prior. The next we hear of him, in 1068, he is abbot at the Cluniac abbey of St Michel-le-Tonnere, a position presumably not congenial to him since we find him back in Montier in 1072, with the rank of ordinary choir-monk. Some months later he is appointed Prior of Saint-Ayoul in Provins, a dependency of Montier-la-Celle, only to abandon this post after less than two years.

By 1074 he has led a group of his companions to the woods of Collan to found a hermitage, and in 1075 moves on to some land given to him by Hugues of Maligny to found the abbey of Molesme.

Despite the comparative lack of reliable historical detail regarding Robert's career and motivations to fill out this bare list of dates, it is difficult not to get a picture of a man of intense feeling whose restlessness and dissatisfaction with the rhythm of Cluniac life prevailing in his day combine with an immense charisma over his fellow monks, the whole seasoned with more than a little confusion over the course of action to pursue. Here we have a man living a life he feels to be too far removed from what St Benedict was talking about 600 years earlier, and determined to take steps to remedy the situation: the Cistercian ideal had been conceived.

One could be forgiven for thinking that the Abbey of Molesme was to provide the perfect setting for this man of piety to put his ideals into practice. His obvious sincerity and genuine desire for a return to the asceticism of the early Benedictine experience attracted numerous postulants to the Abbey. It soon earned itself such a reputation for spiritual efficacy that it became the object of an abundance of donations, becoming increasingly wealthy and powerful, founding over forty priories, cells and hermitages and generally turning into a successful version of the very Cluniac abbeys whose lifestyle it had set out to reject.

While in 1082 the high spiritual tension of Molesme had attracted such fervent idealists as St Bruno, who was inspired by Robert's love of heremitic asceticism to found the Carthusian order after doing his novitiate in the abbey, by 1090 the mass of new recruits and the benefices and donations in money and property flooding in required organizational qualities, or 'managerial' talents as we would call them today, quite beyond the capabilities of Robert and his original band of hermits.

Frustrated in his search for peace, simplicity and nearness to God, Robert's thirst for perfection got the better of him and he moved to Aux, near Riel-les-Eaux, to found a new hermitage and start all over again. But Molesme without Robert had lost its most important attraction, and within a short time the monks had persuaded Robert to return. Molesme in the 1090s is the real birthplace of the Cistercian ideal. After Robert's return, the abbey split into two camps: those who, with Robert, upheld the superiority of the rule of St Benedict over all else, and those, the majority, who insisted on the supremacy of Cluniac usage. This incurred bitter discussion and argument.

A number of the original group of hermits, utterly weary of this state of affairs, left Molesme in 1097 to found a hermitage high in the Alps of Savoie, called St Jean d'Aulps. The charter of Aulps mentions, among other things, that the monk's intention is to adhere strictly to the rule of St Benedict, to the exclusion of any other tenet or dictate. The monks left with the blessing of Robert, and the charter was drawn up by his secretary, one Stephen Harding from Sherborne in Dorset.

It was in the autumn of the same year that Robert's patience ran out. Shamed into action by the resolve of his companions at Aulps, he gathered his most faithful followers around him, including his secretary Stephen, and swept off to demand an audience of Archbishop Hugues of Lyon. To this most staunch supporter of the reforming policies of the current Pope, Gregory VII, he presented his case for founding a new monastery ('*Novum Monasterium*') in strict observance of the rule of St Benedict, openly accusing his own Molesme of slothful negligence and lukewarm adherence to the Benedictine ideal.

The Church at this time was feeling ebullient, thanks to Pope Gregory's recent triumph in the squabble over papal investiture. The Holy Roman Emperor Henry IV had been thoroughly humbled outside the walls of Matilda of Tuscany's castle of Canossa, and perhaps there was a general feeling in church circles that the knife should be driven home while the wound was fresh. Any reform tending to uphold the spirituality of the church and to be seen to do so could only add lustre to the triumphal reign of Pope Gregory and give depth and substance to his recent victory.

Strengthened in their resolve by the enthusiasm shown by Archbishop Hugues, Robert and his band of twenty-one faithful followers took possession, on 21 March 1098, of a small parcel of land some 20 kilometres south of Dijon, given to them for the express purpose of founding on it their *Novum Monasterium*. The nature of the land was distinctly unwelcoming, consisting of dense forest interspersed with marshy bogland,

St Jean d'Aulps, France. Abbey Church, ruins

and there is every reason to believe that this is just what Robert and his followers wanted. The place was called Cîteaux, or *Cistercium* in Latin.

Many theories have been advanced as to the etymology of the word Cîteaux, but the most likely is as always the most banal: it would seem that the site lay '*cis tertium lapidem miliarium*' (just this side of the third milestone) on the old Roman road from Langres to Chalon-sur-Saône. The complete absence of anything stirring about the name is in striking contrast with what was to become a hallmark of Cistercian settlements. Contenting themselves with nothing short of the most inhospitable, isolated, overgrown and generally hostile wildernesses, their radiant faith in God's mercy and their own skills in husbandry, mixed with a dash of presumption and bravado, have given us a litany of names that reads like a poem: La Bénisson-Dieu, Belloc, Val-Benoîte, Bonaygue, Grace-Dieu, La Merci-Dieu, La Colombe, Palais Notre-Dame, Bon-Repos, Clairmont, Lieu-Dieu, Clairmarais, La Clarté-Dieu, Bonnefontaine, Clairefontaine, Beaulieu, Clairlieu and Clairvaux. The same is true outside France: Chiaravalle, Valserena, Acquaformosa, Bonaval, Valparaiso, Valbuena, Valdieu, Mariawald, Marienfeld, Ruhekloster, Baumgartenberg, Bonmont, Vallis Honesta, Zlata Koruna, Paradies, Vale Royal, Dieulacres, Strata Florida, Sweetheart, Mellifont, Belmont.

The new community spent most of the rest of the year building themselves temporary lodgings, clearing the land and sowing essential crops; their spiritual needs were served by an old chapel existing in the vicinity. '*Ora et Labora*' (Pray and Work) had found its true home.

Not many months passed, however, before the monks of Molesme, once more in difficulty without their figurehead, appealed to the Pope to have their abbot returned. The Pope deferred the case to Archbishop Hugues, who in turn deferred it to a synod of local worthies and bishops. Abbot Geoffrey of Molesme resigned to facilitate Robert's return, and Robert was ordered to resume the post. Provision was made for any other monk of Cîteaux to return if he pleased, and a number of them did so. It is significant that the document ordering Robert back to Molesme specifically mentions the 'habitual inconstancy' we had noted in his earlier career, opening the way for Geoffrey to be reinstated as abbot should Robert wander off again. The clause proved an unnecessary precaution, and Robert ended his days peacefully in Molesme in 1111; he was canonized in 1220, and it is only after 1222 that official Cistercian documents start to include his name at the beginning of lists of the Abbots of Cîteaux.

We are told by William of Malmesbury, an English Benedictine monk writing within Robert's lifetime, that Robert returned 'not unwillingly' to Molesme; apparently the order which was to spring from the *Novum Monasterium* he had founded, and which had its roots in his ideals, took over one hundred years to forgive him for what it regarded as his betrayal of the cause.

If we consider for a moment that Robert was into his 70s when Cîteaux was founded, and that the harsh conditions of life there, before any permanent structure had been put up, must have been far more of a burden for him and his contemporaries than for those brothers fired with the ardour of youth, perhaps we can afford him a little more sympathy and understanding than the first Cistercian historians. His humanity may have weakened his resolve at the end, but it is thanks to his vision alone that the seeds were sown which were to change the face of medieval monasticism. The flowering of the Cistercian Order under the steady hand of Stephen Harding and the fertile guidance of Bernard of Fontaines could only have taken root in the furrows ploughed by Robert of Molesme.

A large majority of the original hermits returned to Molesme in Robert's wake, leaving a mere handful to persevere with the ideal. This handful elected Robert's deputy, Prior Alberic, to the abbacy, and it was he who, against all likelihood, strengthened and consolidated the spiritual and material legacy of Robert, encouraging new vocations, adhering strictly to the letter of Benedict's rule, and at the same time dealing with the physical business of setting the abbey on its feet.

Accepting realistically that the first piece of land they had occupied was totally unsuitable for settling, and that no monastic foundation could be expected to survive on it, Alberic promptly moved to a site one kilometre away. Just as unwelcoming and wild as their first piece of land, this one was, however, served by a brook. This is one of Alberic's first recorded decisions, and it is entirely practical, without in any way diminishing the spiritual value of the enterprise. Nothing could better sum up the difference between Robert and his successor. In the entire account of Robert's life, we are not told of a single practical decision he made. Perhaps it was to the good fortune of the Cistercian Order that, after enfusing the foundation with his spiritual idealism, Robert decided to return to Molesme.

Alberic set about consolidating the foundation in numerous ways. It was under him that the abbey's independence was confirmed by the same papal privilege that put the new community under the protection of the

Pope. He personally ensured the benevolence of the Dukes of Burgundy towards the new monastery, negotiating with Duke Odo the donation of the order's first vineyard, Meursault, and with his son and successor Duke Hugh the supply of stone to build the first abbey church.

The abbey church was formally consecrated by the Bishop of Chalon-sur-Saône on 16 November 1106 and dedicated to the Blessed Virgin Mary. In principal, all Cistercian abbey churches ever since that date have been dedicated to the Blessed Virgin Mary. It has been suggested recently that the Cistercians, alone of medieval monastic orders, built their churches in harmony with 'earth forces', an ancient druidic teaching and one closely associated with the powers attributed to underground springs and streams, said to flow from the earth mother or mother goddess. If this is so, then it is surely fitting that the abbey church, the true hub of the monastic complex, should be dedicated to the person who occupies the place of that mother goddess in the Christian tradition.

Alberic's lasting contribution to the Cistercians, however, was undoubtedly his decision to abandon the traditional black garb of the Benedictines and to clothe his small flock in a habit of undyed wool. The rejection of the wordly wealth associated with the Cluniacs inevitably brought with it the inability and unacceptability of purchasing cloth ready woven and dyed black. At the same time a return to a balanced interpretation of Benedict's injunction both to pray and to work meant that early Cistercian communities were self-supporting. Only thus could monks desiring to be cut off from the world fulfill their ambitions in a world largely dominated by monks and monasteries. They reared their own sheep and made their own clothes from undyed wool in a literal interpretation of Benedict's recommendation to wear the 'basest garment possible'. The resulting habit was at first a dirty grey colour; while it was soon bleached white, to represent purity, it was never dyed and to this day the white habit under a black scapular affords instant recognition of the White Monks of popular tradition.

In January 1109, Alberic's death set the stage for the election to the abbacy of Stephen Harding, the man whose genius is responsible for the survival, and indeed for the very existence, of the Cistercian movement in the form in which it left its mark on history. To paraphrase a well-known saying about another genius, Augustus, Stephen Harding 'found Cîteaux just another reformed abbey and left it the head of the first religious order in the true sense of the word'. Nothing like it had ever been seen before.

At the head of a flourishing family of daughter-houses, with a clearly defined manifesto and a full legal constitution, Cîteaux was to become a force for change, and a force to be reckoned with in a world where church and state, from Pope and emperor to bishop and baron, vied to outdo each other in accruing and displaying wealth and power.

Of noble Anglo-Saxon birth, Stephen entered the Abbey of Sherborne, in Dorset, when still a boy. The fate of his family after the Battle of Hastings in 1066 is unknown to us, but it might not be a coincidence that it was in the 1070s that Stephen undertook a pilgrimage to Rome. His original intention might have been to return to his monastery at Sherborne once he had completed the journey, but fate decreed otherwise when it led him along a path that passed by the gates of Molesme. Here, in 1085, he found a haven of spirituality and a safe refuge from a world that to him must have seemed especially troubled.

His sharp mind and penetrating intellect soon brought him to the attention of Abbot Robert, and within a short time he had become a convinced disciple of the man and his ideals. In his travels he cannot have failed to come into contact with the reforms of Giovanni Gualberto and St Romuald in Italy, and the increasingly obvious difficulties encountered by Robert at Molesme must have appeared to him as a challenge to put his experience and organizational skills to good use in helping the saintly abbot achieve his purpose.

By 1109, Stephen was one of the veterans of the group at Cîteaux and probably the one closest in sensibility to Robert's original aims, so it is not unnatural that he was unanimously agreed upon to be the perfect choice for abbot. Essentially likable, kind-natured and possessed of great charm, Stephen's greatest legacy to the Cistercians is the constitutional framework he gave to the order, known as the *Carta Caritatis*, the charter of charity. Oddly, for a document whose impact was so profound and whose fame has echoed down the ages, we have no idea exactly what the original text looked like. The version that has come down to us, and which is believed to contain modifications compared to the original text, cannot be earlier than the second half of the twelfth century, and Stephen died in 1134. However, reference is made repeatedly to the existence of the document throughout the first flowering of daughter-houses which occurred under Stephen from 1112 until his death. So although we have to guess at the text, we can be reasonably certain that it was written within the first eighteen months of Stephen's abbacy and its formulation in his mind probably goes back to his days in Molesme.

It had been proved time and again that for a return to the spirit and the letter of St Benedict's rule to work, good intentions were simply not enough. Stephen himself had been an eye-witness to the very limited success and at times the complete failure of such attempts, and was now personally involved in the front line. His clear and rational vision made it obvious to him that if any such attempt were to be lastingly successful, then some sort of guideline and a set of regulations to govern it were going to have to be laid down. And that is exactly what he did.

The six little pages of flowing Latin prose that make up the *Carta Caritatis* are in effect the constitution of an articulated religious order, regulating the relationship within that order between the various houses comprising it and rooting that relationship in charity. Very little that is new in the document actually concerns the lifestyle of each monk to be observed within the individual monasteries, but then of course Benedict's rule was very specific on that already. A number of modifications were envisaged to bring certain aspects of the rule into line with the spirit of charity, or humanity, on which the edifice of Cîteaux was built. For instance, the practice of accepting child novices forced into the cloister against their will by overburdened, ambitious or uncaring relations was abolished. Of course, the fact that the monks may have found young children in the cloister a distraction may also play a part in this decision. But the fundamental principle which informs the *Carta Caritatis* throughout is that the rule of St Benedict is to be observed rigorously, strictly and as literally as possible. The very reason for the existence of Cîteaux lies in keeping faith with this tenet.

What is revolutionary about the document is the structure imposed on the series of abbeys which were soon to make up the Cistercian family. Modern research has shown that this part, at least formally, is the product of a later hand. But it was a significant part of Stephen's vision that only mutual love and esteem, combined with a benevolent eye to human frailty and gentle correction to guide wanderers back to the true path, could ensure the survival of the ideal. From now on, as the name of the document implies, charity rather than the exercise of power was to be the guiding principle behind the organization of the monastic family, both within each establishment and as a group.

The *Carta Caritatis* instituted the system of visitation of daughter-houses by the mother-house on a regular basis, and provided for the holding of an Annual General Chapter to take place at Cîteaux every year, at which all the abbots were required to be present. It was the first time that a monastic family had been given a family-tree. The abbot of a mother-house could call to order or even depose, for any transgression of the rule, the abbot of any of his abbey's daughter-houses, while he himself could in turn be dismissed by the abbot of his own mother-house. Even the Abbot of Cîteaux itself had to answer to the abbots of the first four foundations.

As is to be expected from a product of the twelfth century, this system shares many elements with the feudal structure, such as the obligation to keep faith with one's overlord and the overlord's duty to dispense justice in his turn to his vassals. However, under the feudal system no one could depose the king, hence the pyramid is perfect and inherently stable, regardless of the downward behaviour of its component members. At Cîteaux the very fact that everyone was keeping an eye on everyone else meant that no one could afford to stray from the prescribed path, since all abbots were merely caretakers. In theory the individual power of the great feudal abbots had been broken, to be replaced by that of the Order.

The figure of the all-powerful feudal abbot of medieval tradition is exemplified by the abbots of Cluny, who in effect governed a virtual empire. It is thus no surprise to learn from William of Malmesbury that Stephen devoted much of his time to upholding the Cistercian reform against attacks by the Cluniacs. Robert of Molesme had already had to sustain such attacks several years earlier and had had to take a defensive stance, maintaining that he and his band were planning nothing more sub-versive than a return to a literal interpretation of the rule of St Benedict. Stephen, however, was altogether more virulent in his tactics, unabashedly attacking Cluniac customs and propounding the superiority of the Cis-tercian life style which could trace its ancestry more directly to the noble lineage of St Benedict. It is here that we find the spirit, if not the letter, of the *Carta Caritatis* at work in Stephen's activity, and thus we can claim with some confidence that the whole Cistercian adventure began as a re-action to Cluny, and that this reaction was crystallized into institutional form under Stephen Harding.

This is an important point to make, since it is often maintained that it was Bernard of Fontaines who initiated the attack on Cluny and its excesses in his famous 'Apologia' of 1124. While it cannot be denied that the discussion grew in scope and power after this date, it is essential to realize

that Bernard, thanks in no small measure to his outstanding command both of Latin prose and of rhetoric, simply championed a cause that had first taken root some forty years earlier. The climax of the conflict came towards the middle of the century and must have held the sweet taste of triumph for the Cistercians. At the height of his powers, Abbot Peter the Venerable of Cluny, whose qualities we have already extolled, not only praised the virtues of Cistercian reform (although he pointedly omitted humility from the list) but actually tried to introduce a few elements of that reform into Cluniac life.

Stephen Harding is also responsible for introducing an element into Cistercian life which was to become a distinguishing feature of the order. It was during Stephen's abbacy that the first 'granges' were acquired to provide the abbey with the means to remain self-supporting. One of Stephen's first acquisitions was the area known as the 'Clos Vougeot'. A 'grange' was in essence a farm situated some distance away from the abbey itself, requiring that a separate cell be set up to manage the estate. Granges were generally up to a day's walking distance from the abbey precinct, thus occasionally requiring its staff to remain absent from the monastery overnight. This of course was hardly compatible with the rule of St Benedict. Indeed there are grounds for thinking that when Benedict spoke of 'labor', what he had in mind was not so much heavy manual labour on the farm as sweeping, cleaning, washing-up, cooking and doing other odd jobs or practising light handicrafts around the cloister.

To solve this dilemma in a manner both consonant with spiritual requirements and of immense practicality (a combination typical of Stephen Harding), the Cistercians institutionalized a practice that had existed casually in a number of Benedictine monasteries for some time.

OPPOSITE ABOVE Great Coxwell, England. Barn: the slit window on the first-floor porch of this grange barn, belonging to the Abbey of Beaulieu, corresponds on the inside to the brother grangiarius' simple living quarters. The word grange, for the Cistercians, applied to the whole farm rather than just the barn, as was the case with other orders. The thirteenth-century barn is still in use

OPPOSITE BELOW Volleron, France. Barn: although the thunder of jet aircraft landing at nearby Charles-de-Gaulle airport has long since put paid to the tranquillity of this Cistercian grange, belonging to the Abbey of Chaalis, the barn at Volleron still fulfills its original function. The wide door on the left was inserted 200 years ago to accommodate large wheeled vehicles; the tower on the right contains a spiral stair leading to the brother grangiarius' living quarters

They gave formal dignity to the figure of the '*conversus*' or lay brother. Lay brothers were normally of less exalted stock than the full choir monks, could neither read nor write, and only took partial vows. They were in effect the agricultural labourers of the monastery and grange, usually far outnumbering the actual choir monks, and the whole west wing of the monastery was given over to them. They acted as a buffer between the monks and the world, acting for them in business and making it unnecessary for them to leave the monastery.

The popularity of such an institution with the peasant classes all over Europe is easily understandable in an age when no one was sure where the next meal would come from. Employment as a lay brother meant a guarantee of a roof over one's head, a dry if somewhat uncomfortable bed, and two meals a day. In exchange for such otherwise unattainable security, all that was required of the lay brother was to work probably no harder than would have been necessary on his own or his feudal lord's land, to attend church services perhaps a little more frequently, which can hardly have been much of a sacrifice in an age where belief in God was seldom questioned, and to forgo the company of women, which was possibly a little more taxing. Surely a small price to pay, however, in return for what was offered? The institution of the lay brothers reached its apogee in the twelfth and early thirteenth centuries, a time of rising population and labour glut. It became the cardinal point on which the future success of Cistercian abbeys rested, and indeed the true decline of the order set in after the Black Death of 1348 had deprived the whole of Europe of the major part of its labour force.

People often express surprise when they learn that the sweeping view up the aisle of a Cistercian abbey church as we see it today would have been impossible during the heyday of the order due to the presence of a rood screen or *jubé*, more often than not a stone wall dividing the church into two quite rigidly distinct sectors, the east end near the high altar and the crossing for the choir monks, and the west end for the lay brothers. This surprise, which owes much to current notions of equality, would have been beyond the understanding of an inhabitant of twelfth-century Christendom where few questioned the position they occupied in the social pecking order. To them it was obvious that God had placed them

OPPOSITE Chiaravalle di Fiastra, Italy. Lay brothers' refectory: the floor tilts imperceptibly inwards so that water used to wash it can flow through draining holes in the flagstones in the central channel which are laid directly over a stream in their given station in society, and living in accordance with God's will, rather than emancipation, was the most important aspiration of twelfth-century man.

The *Novum Monasterium*, just like Molesme a quarter of a century before, quickly attracted numerous novices inspired by its reputation for moral rectitude and religious fervour. Within three years of Stephen being elected abbot, sufficient recruits had arrived at Cîteaux for him to send out a party of twelve monks and their designated abbot to found the first daughter-house. So a group of monks (reflecting in number the apostles of Jesus Christ) set out to build another temple to the rule of St Benedict in a marshy wilderness in the south of the diocese of Chalon-sur-Saône, at a place called La Ferté-sur-Grosne. Cistercian tradition has it that La Ferté was founded in May 1113.

In that same year a young nobleman of the region called Bernard of Fontaines, along with thirty companions including four of his brothers, numerous cousins, uncles and other relations, came knocking on the gate of Cîteaux, asking to be admitted as novices. The future of the order was assured. As we shall see in the next chapter, this man, better known to history as St Bernard of Clairvaux, placed the Cistercian order single-handedly in the forefront of European affairs.

A certain hagiographic tradition has grown up around the figure of St Bernard which claims that the monastery at Cîteaux was all but moribund and would soon have sunk into insignificance had it not been for the arrival of Bernard in time to save it. His powers of resurrection are often portrayed as little short of miraculous. To bolster this picture, his biographers, from the Middle Ages to today, have even gone so far as to falsify the date of his entry to Cîteaux, placing it in 1112 to make the foundation of the first daughter-house at La Ferté appear to have been made possible only by his arrival. This, as we have seen, is untrue and ungenerous to Bernard's predecessors. What cannot be disputed, however, is that Bernard's arrival did give tremendous impulse to the expansion of the order. La Ferté was followed in 1114 by Pontigny, Bernard himself founded Clairvaux in 1115, and Morimond was founded in the same year. By 1119 Preuilly, La Cour-Dieu, Bouras, Cadouin and Fontenay had all been added to the family. By the time Stephen Harding died in 1134, seventy abbots attended the Annual General Chapter. In 700 years of monasticism in Europe, nothing quite like this had ever been seen before.

OPPOSITE ABOVE Badia a Settimo, Italy. Lay brothers' refectory

OPPOSITE BELOW Tintern, Wales. Nave, west end: remains of wall originally dividing lay brothers' nave from aisles are clearly visible

2. Bernard of Fontaines

BERNARD OF FONTAINES was born in 1090 in his father's castle of Fontaines, a small village in Burgundy not far from Dijon. Third child of a family of the minor nobility, vassals of the Dukes of Burgundy, from and for whom they held the castles of Fontaines and Châtillon, Bernard received his early education at home. His mother Aleth, a woman renowned for her piety in the neighbourhood, personally taught him to write and to read from the psalter – as the third son, his father Tescelin had already marked him out for an ecclesiastical career. It was expected, given the excellent family connections with which Bernard was blessed, that he would rise high in the service of Holy Mother Church. One cannot help but muse that while Bernard did indeed rise to the greatest heights, it was possibly not quite in the way his father had originally intended.

At the age of seven, on Christmas Eve 1097, Bernard is said to have had a dream in which the Virgin appeared to him holding the Christ Child in her arms as though He had been born again under Bernard's very eyes. This vision marked the young and obviously impressionable boy deeply, and it was soon after that his parents decided to send him to the school run by the Canons of St Vorles in Châtillon. Initially a timid if very talented pupil, after a year we are told that he had already emerged as something of a leader among his fellow scholars, admired for his silent strength.

He excelled in the study of both sacred and classical texts. It appears that, of the church fathers, St Augustine made a particular impression on him, while Ovid was his favourite among the classical authors. His studies also embraced texts as diverse as the Bible and Boethius, and great emphasis was laid on the study of grammar, rhetoric and dialectic. It is unlikely that the study of the last of these three subjects found much favour with Bernard, in the light of his later differences with Peter Abelard, but it was in these formative years that the kernel of Bernard's mysticism swelled and began to ripen.

To Bernard, knowledge in itself was not a force for evil, as it had been for Peter Damian, the hermit of Fonte Avellana. It became evil when it was divorced from faith. Inspired by his reading of St Augustine, who held that knowledge should be harnessed to faith rather than pursued for its own sake, Bernard was later to write: 'Thus (with Peter Abelard) the human intellect usurps everything to itself, leaving nothing to faith; it wants to go too high in enquiries which go beyond its power'. When reason ruled faith, as it did with Abelard, then Bernard condemned it. 'What do the Apostles teach us? Not to read Plato, nor to turn and return to the subtleties of Aristotle, not always to learn in order never to reach knowledge of truth; they have taught me to live. Do you believe it is a little thing to know how to live? It is a great thing and indeed the greatest.' In an age such as our own, accustomed to acknowledging without question the supremacy of scientific enquiry, this statement may raise a few smiles; we should not, however, so easily discount Bernard's arguably sometimes self-righteous defence of humility against the self-confident assertions of Peter Abelard on the superiority of dialectic. It was this search for humility and the recognition of his own wretchedness in the eyes of God that kindled in him the ability to feel compassion for the misery of others. This awareness was to lead him straight down the path to Cîteaux, the monastery whose whole manifesto centered on charity.

When Bernard reached his sixteenth birthday, it was decided that his formal education was complete and that he should return to take an active part in the running of his father's estates. Just a few days after his return to Fontaines, with the household in a festive mood to celebrate the feast of St Ambrosinianus on 1 September, the family's joy was suddenly and tragically cut short by the death of Lady Aleth. Bernard was shattered. He had been much closer to his mother than was usual in those days, and this sudden loss, just when he had been looking forward to spending much more time in her company, marked him deeply. His later devotion to the Blessed Virgin has often been seen as a projection of the adoration he had for his mother, and in years to come he admitted that whatever he had accomplished he owed to his determination to fulfill his mother's desires.

Lady Aleth's death represented a turning point in Bernard's life. Unsure how to pursue his mystical ideal, he was subjected to the contrasting advice of his father and his many brothers. His father suggested that he go to study in Germany, after which he could return to serve at the court of the Dukes of Burgundy in Dijon, as a first stepping-stone in his

Sénanque, France. South transept. It was not long before the bare interiors of many abbey churches began to get cluttered with the tombs of benefactors, who insisted on being buried as close to the high altar as possible. The tomb in the picture is that of the Seigneur de Vénasque, mid-thirteenth century

OPPOSITE Le Thoronet, south-transept chapels from south aisle ecclesiastical career. His brothers, impatient with his dithering, summoned him to their aid in helping the Duke of Burgundy besiege Grancey. Bernard felt sure that neither of these paths was the right one for him, but for lack of a better occupation he took himself off to Grancey to join his brothers. On the way, his mother appeared to him in a dream and reproached him for not showing enough strength of character. He replied that her death had caused him such a grievous sense of loss that he felt incapable of making any decision. His mother advised him to go into a chapel nearby and pray, and it was in that chapel that a light parted the clouds in his mind and he knew that his path would lead to the gates of Cîteaux.

Cîteaux at the time had already acquired a reputation for honesty and rigour in the region, but was considered for the most part a fringe experience and not one that would allow any of its adherents to climb the ladder of a rewarding ecclesiastical career.

When Bernard reached Grancey, he only admitted his plans to his uncle Gaudry; afraid of his brothers' scorn, he lied to them that he was unable to take part in the siege since he had made up his mind to go on pilgrimage to Jerusalem. This sounded fairly plausible, given his known religious bent, and the recapture of the Holy City from the Saracens at the end of the first crusade in 1099 was still fresh in everyone's memory. This, his only recorded lie, is based on a dream he entertained for the whole of his life and never realized. In view of the fervour with which Bernard was to preach the second crusade some thirty-five years later, it is likely that this tale did contain a kernel of truth, and that he would very much have liked to go to Jerusalem. Yet despite extensive travelling throughout Christendom and the fact that, during his lifetime, the Latin Kingdom of Jerusalem was at its safest and most easily accessible from the West, Bernard never went to the Holy Land. His close involvement with the Knights Templar is further proof of his passion for the crusading ideal, and modern research has suggested that the plan of every Cistercian monastery is an attempt to reproduce the Celestial Jerusalem, Augustine's City of God, on earth. However that may be, Bernard never saw the earthly Jerusalem.

His uncle Gaudry, inspired by the fervour with which Bernard revealed to him his true plans, was unable to keep the secret for long and soon announced his intention of joining Bernard in his decision to enter the novitiate at Cîteaux. His true purpose revealed, Bernard quickly displayed his natural qualities as a leader and set about convincing his brothers to adhere to the enterprise too. By the time the family had arrived back in Châtillon, Bartholomew, Guy, Andrew and Gerard who, though wounded and taken prisoner during the siege and miraculously escaped, had all decided to take up with their brother. It was thus that a band of thirty aspiring novices, all friends and relations who had fallen under Bernard's charismatic spell, arrived in the spring of 1113 at the gates of Cîteaux, asking to be received into the monastery, to pursue their search for God in the fellowship of the austere White Monks of Abbot Stephen.

At Cîteaux, Bernard was finally in his element. While he felt more keenly than most the physical deprivations caused by the severity of the rule of Cîteaux, to the extent that he fell ill early on and never really recovered to the end of his life, his spiritual talents blossomed. Always willing to learn in humility from Abbot Stephen and his fellow monks, Bernard soon became one of the most eloquent interpreters and defenders of the message of Cîteaux. Stephen Harding was not slow to recognize Bernard's exceptional qualities. When he received a request from Count Hugh of Champagne in 1115 to found a monastery on his lands, he chose the twenty-five-year-old Bernard to lead the party of monks he was proposing to send to comply with Count Hugh's invitation, and to become abbot of the new foundation. The land Count Hugh offered was, not surprisingly, a forbidding piece of marshy bog in the midst of a barren wilderness. Bernard decided that it would be called Clairvaux, the clear valley, where, with God's help, the monks would make a second paradise out of land that no normal person would even have attempted to cultivate.

Bernard was to remain Abbot of Clairvaux for the rest of his life. He had found his roost. And yet in the thirty-seven years of life left to him, he spent more time away from his monastery than in it. He was looking for, and had found, total seclusion from the world, a desert like that of the early Christian hermits in which to pursue his ideal of oneness with God in the exclusive company and charitable fellowship of like-minded souls. After two years, even his father and his youngest brother joined him at Clairvaux. And yet almost despite himself he couldn't keep himself from playing an active and indeed dominating role in the affairs of his time. It is little wonder he defined himself as the chimera of his century.

His reputation for sanctity soon spread throughout France, and within three years of Clairvaux being established, there were sufficient inmates to permit the foundation of its first daughter-house, Trois-Fontaines in Champagne, not far from the town of Vitry-le-François. His writings

Noirlac, France. Most abbeys in the early days would have resembled an anonymous (but prosperous) collection of farm buildings

OPPOSITE Noirlac, France. South aisle, looking west

attracted the attention of the great all over Christendom in an age which, in the words of Lekai, 'was desperately in search of an able and competent authority'. In the Holy Roman Empire, the death of Emperor Henry V without a clear heir, in 1125, had left the land in the turmoil that was to engender the feuds of the Guelph and Ghibelline factions. In England a similar situation had developed with the death of Henry I Beauclerc, the last son of the Conqueror. His daughter Empress Matilda, widow of Emperor Henry V, had been challenged in her claim to the succession by her cousin Count Stephen of Blois, giving rise to a civil war that was to last fifteen years.

In France, King Louis VI, the Fat, had left a weak-willed and inexperienced young boy to follow him, having made sure before he died that the boy married the wealthiest heiress in Christendom. What the king had been unable to do was to judge the wife he was thrusting on his son, known to history as Louis the Monk, in any other way than on hearsay. The Lady Eleanor of Aquitaine, whom Bernard was to get to know very well during the course of his career, was quite the most extraordinary woman of her century, and far too strong for poor young Louis VII. History knows her as the wife of two kings and the mother of another two kings and two queens. Bernard was to find this tempestuous lady more than a little disconcerting.

In Italy the prosperous cities of the north were taking full advantage of the chaos to assert their independence. Emperor Frederick Barbarossa's sack of Milan is the most eloquent testimony of the sort of retribution they attracted. In Rome rival factions managed to elect two rival popes on the same day that Pope Honorius II died in 1130. It could be said, and indeed it was said, that God had turned his face away from the world.

The nobility, both lay and ecclesiatical, of France held a council at Etampes to decide which pope it served their best interests to support, and Bernard was called in to advise. In the end it was his eloquence in favour of Innocent II and his condemnation of the violence of Anacletus II that carried the day for the former. Having persuaded the French of the sanctity and righteousness of Innocent's claims, Bernard now felt he had to see his task through. He persuaded King Henry I of England, when the latter monarch was visiting his domains in Normandy, to lend his support to Innocent's cause, and spent the better part of the next eight years convincing every one else in Europe who mattered to put their weight behind the man he regarded as God's elected. His fiery letters, draughted in a consciously elegant and beautiful Latin prose, sped to and fro between the chanceries of half Christendom. Between 1130 and 1131 he personally accompanied Innocent on a campaign which took him to the four corners of modern France putting his talents of persuasion at the service of the papal cause.

In 1132 he travelled south to uphold the cause before the assembled magnates of the Midi. The next year he was doing the same in Genoa, then in Pisa, and finally he accompanied Innocent to Rome. In 1135 he took part in the Diet of Bamberg, and in the same year he was again in Pisa for the great Council meeting, after which he toured the Po valley from Milan to the coast, preaching in favour of Pope Innocent. Finally, in 1137, he was called to Rome by the college of cardinals to assist in arbitration, and in 1138 the schism came to an end, with the deposition of Anacletus and the victory of Innocent II. In view of the travelling conditions of the day, we cannot but admire Bernard's boundless energy in favour of a cause he championed with passion, but what is most to his credit is that, wherever he went, he actually succeeded in bringing all his audience round to his way of thinking. So persuasive an orator was he that it is said 'mothers locked their sons away and wives their husbands' when he was in the vicinity preaching to attract postulants.

Bernard's charisma was such that throughout his travels, ostensibly given over to the promotion of Innocent II's cause, he won over recruits to his monastic ideal, both among aspiring novices or existing monastic communities and among the landed gentry. Wherever he went he not only fired men with the enthusiasm to join the order of Cîteaux but was continually offered land on which to build new monasteries. The fact that the Cistercians purposely sought out land that was otherwise unprofitable may have influenced the generosity of many benefactors, such as the Lord of Marigny who donated an especially inhospitable piece of land he owned in the valley of the Arvault in Burgundy for the purpose of founding the abbey of La Bussière, which even today is particularly difficult to get to. The act of donation states that Marigny's gift was made to ensure the salvation of his soul. It cannot have been purely incidental that by the same act he turned some useless land in one fell swoop into a highly profitable agricultural estate.

Within his own lifetime, Bernard personally founded and sponsored the foundation of or reformed some sixty-five abbeys in Europe. During the eight years in which he travelled through France and Italy on Innocent

Wettingen, Switzerland. Stained-glass window in the cloister arcade tracery:
St Bernard at the feet of the Madonna and Child

Tiglieto, Italy. The sorry state of the chapter house in the first abbey founded outside France. Since the photo was taken, the bas-relief has been stolen

II's behalf, Clairvaux became the mother of Chiaravalle di Milano, Chiaravalle della Colomba, Le Tre Fontane, Fossanova and Sant'Andrea di Sestri in Italy, Bonmont in Switzerland, Eberbach and Himmerod in Germany, Rievaulx and Fountains in England, Les Dunes in Flanders, Moreruela in Spain, and in his native France, of Vaucelles, Vauclair, Grace-Dieu, Noirlac, La Bénisson-Dieu and Clairmarais.

Meanwhile, the other daughters of Cîteaux were not idle. Pontigny had founded Bourras, Fontainejean, Jouy, St Sulpice and Quincy during the same period, and the old-established abbey of Cadouin had voluntarily placed itself under the Cistercian wing. Morimond had been particularly fertile in Alsace, Franche-Comté and the territory of the Holy Roman Empire, founding Bellevaux and La Crête by 1121 and Camp and Ebrach within the same decade. Heiligenkreuz near Vienna followed soon after.

While Cîteaux itself counted relatively few direct daughter-houses after it had founded the first four, it became the recipient of an extraordinary transfer in 1147 when the entire recently-founded order of Savigny made itself over to the mother-house of the Cistercians. This order included twenty-nine fully-fledged abbeys, among which Buildwas, Byland and Furness are the best known in England, and Savigny, Les Vaux-de-Cernay, Aulnay and La Trappe in France. One of the smallest of the shoots off the monastic family tree belongs to La Ferté, Cîteaux's first daughter-house, and yet it is to this abbey that is ascribed the first foundation outside the boundaries of modern France. As early as 1120 a stalwart group of twelve monks with their designated abbot and accompanying group of lay-brothers set off across the Alps to found Santa Maria di Tiglieto in the diocese of Genoa in Northern Italy.

A large proportion of the monks that peopled all these new foundations came from the intelligentsia of twelfth-century society. In the early years at Clairvaux, students and teachers from the famous school of Châlons flocked to the abbey to listen to Bernard's sermons, and later, when he travelled to Rheims, Liège and Paris, the same phenomenon repeated itself. It was in Paris that he first came into conflict with that other great master of theology and rhetoric, Peter Abelard. Bernard was a mystic, Abelard a rationalist, there was no common ground between them. Abelard took an almost sensual delight in his own powers of reasoning, in the brilliance of his intellectual abilities, in his capacity to be a thorn in the side of the establishment, and even in his success with women. He 'feared no repulse from whatever woman he might deign to honour with his love'. He also found great enjoyment in drawing away others' students, and in the end it was his capacity to irritate and antagonize his peers and his superiors that proved his downfall. Unsparing of his adversaries, he could expect no quarter. Abelard was the dominant intellectual figure of his day, but he could not resist the temptation to be controversial. In his arrogance, he was always right and, while it is thanks to him that Paris University became the foremost centre of theology and dialectic of the Middle Ages, his voice was out of place in a world thirsty for the unquestioning spiritual certainties of St Bernard.

When Abelard finally came to grief at the Council of Sens in 1140, it was Bernard and his fellow Cistercian William of St Thierry who were among the most vehement in demanding his condemnation. It has become quite fashionable to portray Abelard as the sensitive, almost modern free-thinker, sacrificed like a lamb on the altar of St Bernard's intransigent and often obtuse defense of orthodoxy, but what is often overlooked is the reconciliation which took place between the two at Cluny just prior to Abelard's death, under the aegis of Abbot Peter the Venerable. However misguided, Bernard's intention in opposing Abelard had been that Abelard should see the error of his ways. Bernard would never have countenanced, and certainly did not approve of, the appalling punishment meted out to Peter Abelard for his affair with Héloïse.

Whatever he may have felt about Abelard's errors, both theological and human, he was always moved in his relations with the man by the ideal of charity. He sincerely believed that Abelard was wrong and, given his charisma, a danger to the Church at a time when the Church needed bolstering. On a personal level he had no objections.

Two works composed by Bernard in his mature years give us an insight into the sort of man he was and the ideals which moved him. At the age of thirty-eight he wrote the rule for the Knights Templar and at forty-five he began his sermons on King Solomon's Song of Songs. It is clear from the very different nature of these two documents that Bernard was unaware of any natural incompatibility between fervent admiration of the hardy and ruthless Knights Templar and impassioned devotion to the beautiful and delicate biblical poem. Bernard's good faith is never in doubt, however, and the link between two such seemingly irreconcilable facets of the Christian experience may after all not be so hard to discern. Bernard shared with Solomon that quality common to all mystics that uses a sensual vocabulary to describe spiritual union with the deity. While

Quincy, France. The chapter house is now a cowshed

OPPOSITE San Giusto, Italy. Crypt. Crypts are generally absent from Cistercian churches, but where the order took over existing abbeys from the Benedictines or others it rarely implemented major architectural changes. This crypt was probably built in the eighth to ninth century using recycled classical columns

the life of a hermit was ideally devoted to accomplishing this union, the concept was not absent from the sort of monastery that Bernard was busy setting up, a reflection on earth of the celestial Jerusalem. Bernard's manifesto for redemption which eventually filled Christendom with hundreds of small earthly Jerusalems could hardly wash its hands of the defense of the real thing. It is interesting, in this regard, that the Knights Templar took their name from and made their headquarters in the Temple built by the author of the Song of Songs.

In the same year that Bernard was laying the foundation stone of his abbey's first daughter-house, there came to fruition a project which had been evolving for some years in the heads of a handful of knights in the capital of the newly conquered Latin Kingdom of Jerusalem. This group of veteran Frankish warriors, under the leadership of Hugh de Payens, and counting Bernard's uncle André de Montbard in their number, approached King Baldwin II with a proposition. It was their intention to form a military religious order. Nothing of the sort had ever been heard of before, and indeed to many seemed a contradiction in terms. The word 'crusader' was completely unknown to those who took part in the conquest of Jerusalem in 1099, and even the concept of 'soldiers of Christ' was alien to them. They were, and defined themselves as, simply pilgrims. They were armed for the good reason that the aim of their pilgrimage was to recapture the holy places from an armed foe, the infidel Saracens.

While many of those, especially among the nobility, who joined the first crusade were motivated by faith and greed to the same degree, no one had apparently thought much beyond the recapture of Jerusalem or considered the need to defend the Holy Land on a permanent basis once the object of the pilgrimage had been achieved. King Baldwin of Jerusalem immediately grasped the implications behind the offer of this well-intentioned band of soldiers and lodged them in a wing of his palace, the mosque of Al-Aqsa on the Temple Mount. Ostensibly, the task these knights set themselves was to serve as armed convoys for pilgrims on their travels within the Holy Land, which was still, though conquered, a predominantly moslem-populated and thus potentially hostile country. Their phenomenal growth as an Order (paralleled only by that of the Cistercians), their immense wealth in later years and their obvious expansion beyond their initial purpose coupled with their heroic end have encouraged much speculation as to the real nature of the Knights Templar.

We will probably never know the whole truth about this enigmatic brotherhood, but certainly St Bernard's imagination was fired by their zeal. In 1128, at the Council of Troyes organized by Count Hugh of Champagne, the first patron of the Abbey of Clairvaux and a member of the Templars, Bernard was called upon and enthusiastically agreed to draw up a rule for the new order. Over and above the monastic vows of poverty, chastity and obedience, and the practice of fasting and abstinence, it was enjoined upon the brethren to attend Mass three times a week. Each knight was further required to swear to dedicate his life to the defence, with all his strength, of 'our belief in the unity of the Godhead and the mystery of our faith'. In practical terms he promised to cross the sea as often as necessary and in total obedience to the Grand Master of the Order to aid and bring succour to kings and princes engaged in the holy struggle against the infidel. He was forbidden to retreat or surrender even if the odds be three to one against him. He had to be at least the son of a knight, legitimate, free of all debt and a bachelor or a widower. The proviso that was to have the most lasting and widespread effect was undoubtedly that which specified that no postulant could be under twenty-one years of age. This gradually came to be accepted as the age of majority by society as a whole, and was to remain so for almost 800 years.

That Bernard felt the Templars to be the fighting arm of his own Cistercian order, or at least to be inspired by exactly the same ideal of poverty and other-worldliness, is indicated by his letter to Hugh on learning that he had renounced his title of count in favour of his nephew Thibaut, and had embraced the ideals of the Temple. He writes: 'If for God's cause you have turned from count to knight and from rich to poor, we congratulate you on your advancement. For this is the work of God's right hand'. In a pamphlet entitled *De Laude Novæ Militiæ* (On the Praise of the New Knighthood), Bernard condemns what he calls the effeminacy of current knightly practice, denouncing those knights who bedeck their horses with silk, stud their bridles with gold and precious stones, grow their hair long and wear long floating silken tunics which hamper their vision and impair their freedom of movement. How much worthier, he claims, are the 'Knights of God, with their discipline and unqualified obedience. Each one wears the dress given to him, none goes in search of fine food or garments according to his whim. The Templar is content with what is most necessary, shunning anything superfluous. Impudent words, senseless occupations and immoderate laughter are unknown to him. He despises mimes and jugglers, dirty songs and the performance of

Badia a Settimo, Italy. Lay brothers' refectory: capital portraying abbey benefactor

OPPOSITE Alcobaça, Portugal. Nave, based on Clairvaux

buffoons, all these are vanity and inane folly. He cuts his hair short, bathes rarely and is dirty and hirsute, tanned by his hauberk and by the sun'. In these vibrant words of praise, it is not difficult to hear the echo of Bernard's condemnation of Cluniac excesses in the cloister. The life style he envisages for the Templars reflects the austerity of his own order, save in regard to their diet. As fighters, they needed meat and were permitted to drink wine, at the discretion of the master, with their evening meal.

Bernard's insistence in this tract on avoiding the superfluous immediately strikes a note of recognition in the modern reader familiar with Cistercian architecture, and it is ironic that the treatise should have been composed in the ornate Latin prose which was his most effective tool. For Bernard, the beauty of *compositio* was alone worthy of the grave and perfect harmony which is the image and reflection of God. Of all the writings of St Bernard, his skill in the art of Latin composition is shown to best advantage in his sermons on the Song of Songs, the spiritual testimony of love seeking nuptial union with the Deity.

This sublime text combines at once the thousand-year-old tradition of Christianity (and indeed Bernard has been called the last of the Church Fathers) with the first germs of a modern, psychological approach to religion. A cardinal work in the development of Christian thought, the sermons, in the words of Father Bouyer, 'plunge to the source of the Scriptures, like the ancient Fathers, in a way that was not to be seen again. Like the Fathers, Bernard sees Christianity with a single sweeping glance, and monasticism is an integral part of that Christianity'. But, like all great creators who influence their century to the point where it seems they embody it, it is what Bernard concedes spontaneously to the spirit of his time which enables him to play such a crucial part in forming it. All the sensibility of the twelfth century, which in less than a hundred years was to transform through its literature the very conception that man had of his humanity, is enshrined in the sermons on the Song of Songs. With this sensibility, it is the awareness of self, the subjectivity in which the spirit of the modern age is born, that Bernard baptises and thrusts upon the stage of western civilisation. The 'theology of mysticism' based on the

OPPOSITE ABOVE Les Vaux-de-Cernay, France. Nave, looking west

OPPOSITE BELOW Fontenay, France. One of the two twin-light windows used by representatives of the lay brothers to follow discussions relating to any abbey business which might concern them. It was forbidden to lay brothers actually to attend chapter incontrovertible facts of redemption and grace revealed by the Word of God, gives way to the 'psychology of mysticism' which was to reach its climax with the breathtaking visions of St Teresa of Avila and St John of the Cross. The twelfth-century renaissance owes at least as much to the deep soul searching of St Bernard as it does to Queen Eleanor of Aquitaine's fabled courts of love.

In the 1140s the proliferation of Cistercian abbeys throughout Europe was reaching such proportions that there was reputedly not a corner of Christendom left where it was possible to walk ten miles without meeting a white habit. The four first-born were still prodigiously founding, and their daughters, now into the third and fourth generations, were outdoing their parents. This was the decade which saw the birth of Rufford and Roche, Kirkstead and Woburn in the British Isles, Fiastra and Follina, Sambucina and Casamari in Italy, La Noé, Le Pin, L'Etoile and Froidmont in France, Schönau, Otterberg and Viktring, in the Holy Roman Empire. Fitero, Veruela and Huerta in Spain, Silvacane, Fontfroide and Franquevaux in Provence, all belong to this period, as well as the first foundations in Scandinavia, Alvastra and Nydala, and in Ireland, Mellifont and Bective.

While it is true, as is often claimed, that this rapid expansion was due to the excess of postulants which forced abbeys to found daughter-houses or risk anarchy, there is also an element of fashion which should not be disregarded. The Cistercians, from a band of well-meaning hermits lost in the depths of Burgundy, had grown into the most authoritative religious community in Europe. It was natural that royalty and nobility wanting to found a monastery should turn to the most fashionable order of the moment, whose prayers were esteemed to be the most efficacious.

But this could create problems. In 1189 the Annual General Chapter reiterated that each house should contain at least twelve monks, which presumably indicates that some fell short of this number. By the end of the century Bonlieu, San Sebastiano and Ląd were in danger of being demoted to the status of granges, while Falleri, San Giusto di Tuscania and Sala were noted as having fewer than the required number of monks. These were, however, the exceptions, and while we can have no reliable idea about the exact population of the individual monasteries, it cannot be far from the truth to say that by the 1190s there were over 20,000 Ciscercian monks and lay brothers in Europe and the Latin Kingdom of Jerusalem.

As far back as 1124, when the reputation of Cluny was at its lowest ebb after the appalling mismanagement of Abbot Pons of Melgueil, Bernard had felt the time was right to deliver his fatal thrust at the corruption of the black monks, contained in a letter to William of St Thierry known as the *Apologia*. As we shall see later, this letter unwittingly laid down the canons, never otherwise formally enshrined in the statutes, of what was to become the Cistercian style in art and architecture. Its purpose in the eyes of the writer, however, was to prove once and for all the superiority of the Cistercian way of life over the 'usages' of Cluny. He claims that the Cistercians are 'the only monks with any virtue, more saintly than any others, the only monks to live in conformity with the Rule; so far as other monks are concerned, they are simply transgressors of the Rule ... All monks who make their profession according to the Rule must observe it to the letter, without any dispensation whatsoever'. What Bernard was attempting to do was to make the white of the Cistercian habit seem even brighter against the black of the rich, pompous and easy-going Cluniacs. The Cistercians alone were the true heirs to the Gregorian reform, poor in Christ, living off the fruits of their own hard work, renouncing the world and living apart from it, in poverty and austerity, simple in dress and diet, living in unadorned buildings and zealous in their asceticism. Bernard was not alone in championing this lifestyle. The theme was taken up by St Ailred of Rievaulx in his *Speculum Caritatis*, and some years later, with all the passion of a convert, by a former Cluniac who had recently joined the Cistercians, one Isung of Prüfening, in his *Dialogue Between a Cluniac and a Cistercian*.

As self-proclaimed vessels of the Gregorian reform, it was a triumph for the Cistercians, and for Bernard in particular, when a monk of Clairvaux was elected Pope with the name of Eugene III, in 1145. But the Christian world which greeted the election of the new Pope was shocked to its very foundations by the news which came from the east. On Christmas Eve of the previous year, the Saracen leader Nur-ed-Din had captured the Christian citadel of Edessa in the Latin Kingdom. Queen Melissenda of Jerusalem sent urgent pleas to the princes of Christendom for help in defending her throne and the Kingdom against this new threat. The first crusade had succeeded thanks to the disunity of the infidel factions, but now the Arab armies had united and the only way the Latin Kingdom could survive was for the forces of Christendom to present an equally united front and send a massive army to the Middle East to counter the Arab hosts.

Pope Eugene was instantly sensitive to this appeal, and in this showed himself to be a true son of St Bernard. He begged Bernard to use his powers of persuasion to preach the crusade, and naturally Bernard didn't delay. He spent the next two years, from 1146 to 1147, haranguing the crowds from France to Germany, rallying the forces of Christendom for this great adventure.

With the approval of his spiritual protégé King Louis VII of France, and to the initial displeasure of the latter's wife, Queen Eleanor of Aquitaine, Bernard organized an assembly at Vézelay for Easter 1146 during which he would proclaim the holy cause. The news that Bernard was to preach brought listeners from all over the kingdom. Louis had himself vowed to take the cross at the end of the previous year but his attempt to fire the nobility with something of his own enthusiasm had proved a failure, and so he appeared in full support of his spiritual mentor at the assembly, ensuring that it was seen that the venture had the weight of his authority behind it. What Louis probably failed to realize was that Bernard actually carried more authority than he did and, where Louis had failed, Bernard once again succeeded. Even Eleanor vowed, at Vézelay, to take the cross and accompany her husband and his army on crusade. Her behaviour on that crusade is another story altogether.

To his joy, Bernard was able to write to the Pope a few days later: 'You ordered, I obeyed, and the authority of him who gave the order has made my obedience fruitful. I opened my mouth; I spoke; and at once the crusaders have multiplied to infinity. Villages and towns are now deserted. You will scarcely find one man for every seven women. Everywhere you see widows whose husbands are still alive'.

Fired by the success of the assembly at Vézelay, Bernard travelled around Burgundy, Flanders, Alsace and Lorraine, the Rhineland, where he was invited by the Archbishop of Cologne, then to Frankfurt, Freiburg, Schaffhausen, Basle and Lake Constance. At Speyer he convinced King Conrad to join the crusade, and everywhere people flocked in their hundreds. That the crusade got off the ground at all is thanks to his magnetic powers of persuasion and charismatic eloquence. There was nothing of the ranting fanatic about his sermons however. He was the first to guard against the excesses that his enthusiasm might spark off in a half-starved population. When a deranged Cistercian monk called Rudolf began to encourage the massacre of Jews in the Rhineland, Bernard immediately called him to order, chased him back to his monastery and confined him there. A contemporary Jewish chronicler, whom it would be difficult to suspect of bias, says of Bernard: 'Without this just man sent by God, we should all have perished'.

When the crusade proved a failure, and the armies of Christendom returned to the west defeated and disorganized, Bernard was heard to remark, on being told many laid the blame at his door, that he preferred the blame to fall on him than on God: 'If the blindness, avarice and mistrust of men has turned a sure victory into a humiliating defeat, then they only have their sins to blame for it. If in their arrogance they cannot see this, then let them blame me.' While perhaps a little extreme and couched in the language of his century, this perspicacious comment is fairly near the truth. The second crusade failed principally because its commanders could agree on nothing from the moment they set out in 1147 until they returned two years later.

Immensely saddened by this setback, Bernard returned to Clairvaux and dedicated his time to writing his last great work, the *De Consideratione*, a masterpiece of Latin prose dedicated to his erstwhile pupil who had risen to the papacy. Essentially a guide to avoiding the errors into which any Pope might fall in his humanity, it reflects his experience with the second crusade when he sustains that failure must be accepted as a judgement of God. The work is in effect Bernard's spiritual legacy to the world, a summary of his entire life consecrated to God and the Church. Some still feel it has relevance today: Pope John XXIII habitually had it read to him at meal times.

Bernard made one further sortie from Clairvaux, in 1153, when he was called to Lorraine to help prevent a massacre that was about to take place in Metz, where two opposing factions sought control of the city. Both sides listened to him in awe and respect, and the conflict was averted, but the effort proved too much for Bernard. Old at sixty-three, in a world where average life expectancy was not much more than thirty-five and the austerity of Cistercian life reduced even that to twenty-eight, ill and worn out by constant travelling, Bernard made his way painfully back to his beloved Clairvaux where, on 20 August 1153, he died.

At the time of his death the Cistercian abbeys in Europe numbered almost 350. Of these he had personally founded or provided for the foundation of sixty. From Ireland to Sicily, from Spain to the Baltic, no corner of Christendom had been left untouched by the tidal wave of the Cistercian spiritual revolution which stemmed from Clairvaux.

3. The Abbey: Foundation, Construction, Layout and Resources

WHEN A PATRON decided to endow an abbey, he would first apply to the authorities of whichever order he had chosen to favour. If his application was acceptable, and with Cîteaux this was not automatically the case, the Annual General Chapter would empower one or usually two abbots from neighbouring monasteries to carry out a survey of the site. In their quest for solitude, they had promulgated a strict ruling that no abbey was to be situated within 24 kilometres (15 miles) of another. Given the immense spaces available in the under-populated Europe of the late eleventh and early twelfth centuries, this rule might appear unnecessary, but one of the characteristics of the twelfth century is the growth in population and the drive to bring under cultivation vast areas of forest, marsh and flooded coastline. In fact we hear of cases where the new arrivals, in their determination not to sacrifice their ideal of solitude, actually created the desert they sought, transplanting entire villages in order to take possession of the land offered them. The phenomenal growth and popularity of the order also accounted for a number of internal difficulties arising. Byland Abbey in Yorkshire had to be resited four times, over a space of nearly forty years, before it finally took firm root in 1177. Its second site had been immediately contested by the Cistercian monks of Rievaulx who complained that the new foundation was so near to them they could hear its bells ringing and confused them with their own.

Once the foundation had been approved, the ground had to be prepared to receive the abbey buildings. As soon as the colony of twelve monks, with their designated abbot and a handful of lay brothers had arrived at the site, they set about clearing and draining the land on which the buildings were to rise. Temporary wooden accommodation was usually erected immediately after a timber or rough stone chapel had been built. Worshipping God was the monks' primary purpose in life, and took precedence over everything else. It is not known exactly who did what in terms of design and construction of the abbey church and monastery but, while there are undeniable features common to Cistercian architecture from Ireland to the Lebanon, it seems unlikely that the choir monks themselves played any dominant role in the work. Certainly they inspired the design, and most probably lent a hand in a menial capacity, consonant with their aspiration to humility.

The construction work proper, however, appears to have been entrusted to travelling teams of skilled masons, who moved from site to site and lived separately from the monks in their own lodges. They would have been given help by the lay brothers, but we must not forget that it never took less than five years to complete just the bare bones of the monastery. During that time masons, choir monks and the lay brothers themselves had to be fed and clothed, so it is not unreasonable to suggest that they spent most of their time doing what they were constitutionally engaged to do, namely clear the land, drain the marshes and generally make the site suitable for farming.

The abbey church was the first building to go up, starting with the east end. Cistercian abbeys were always oriented, the high altar set towards the east (towards Jerusalem), unless some natural impediment prevented this. Thus, even in the rare cases where the façade is not facing the sunset, it is commonly referred to as the west front. The abbey was built over a number of years, with work out of doors usually limited to the spring and summer months. The master mason would be assisted by the senior carpenter and the plumber who was responsible for lead and glass work. A plumb line was used to ensure that the walls went up straight, and much use was made of set square and compass. The stone tended to arrive already shaped, and marked with the mason's mark in the quarry since masons were paid on a piece-work rather than an hourly basis.

As the church walls got higher, wooden scaffolding was erected and primitive cranes used to raise the stone. Arches and vaults were built over supporting wood frames which were removed once the mortar had set. Made at ground level, roof sections were hoisted to the roof, placed in position and covered with lead and tiles. Once the roof, which had been built in sections on the ground, was in position, the rest of the work on the inside could be finished unhurriedly whatever the weather.

Valserena, Italy. The absence of a separate bell tower was compensated in the thirteenth and fourteenth centuries by the development of splendid bell housings rising above the crossing

OPPOSITE Commelles, France. Brick-oven: many of the bricks used to build the Abbey of Chaalis (of which Commelles was a grange) were baked in this oven

After the church had been completed, work proceeded on the lay brothers' quarters, then on the chapter house, monks' day-room and dormitory, and finally on the refectory, kitchen and warming-house wing. The cloister, usually a wooden lean-to structure replaced only later by stone arcading, completed the picture. The pattern is the same for every single one of the hundreds of Cistercian abbeys built throughout Europe in the Middle Ages. Only the vocabulary varies, and then much less than one would expect in a world where style and design were passed on by drawings and word of mouth or a picture in the mind's eye alone. Each Cistercian abbey is a masterpiece produced by the synthesis of the skills of a master mason and his crew, trained to work in the local material and using the local idiom, with the rigid directives of an abbot and his monks dedicated to reproducing their beloved Cîteaux wherever they went, in the spirit and in the stone.

And yet what is it in Cistercian abbeys that sets them apart from the rest? The layout of a Cistercian abbey, apart from one or two details, is shared by most of the other religious orders of the period, by cathedrals and collegiate churches, Cluniacs, Premonstratensians and Augustinians alike. In the words of Van der Meer, whose beautifully illustrated and acutely intelligent study of the Cistercian order *Atlas de l'Ordre Cistercien* is now sadly out of print and rarely found even in antiquarian or specialist book shops, 'the originality (of Cistercian architecture) lies solely in simplicity taken to its ultimate consequences, especially in the abbey church. The church, the jewel of the complex everywhere else, is here the plainest element: it is in the church that the break with tradition is most evident'.

While the Cistercians' approach to ornament was dictated by their desire that nothing should distract them from their devotion to the worship of God, they had nothing against the decoration of churches *per se*. St Bernard was fully aware of the positive effect of majesty on the sometimes unruly populace, and the frescoed or painted stories from the Bible or the Lives of the Saints were often the only means whereby the illiterate congregation could find visual comfort in the Word of God. They propounded their philosophy fiercely, but only intended it to apply to themselves and their fellow monks. Ascetics, they required ascetic churches which, unlike the churches of most other monastic orders, were not open to the laity.

Had a Cluniac monk walked into one of their churches in the twelfth century, he would have been utterly dumbfounded. Again Van der Meer

OPPOSITE Eberbach, Germany. South aisle

puts it succinctly when he says that our hypothetical Cluniac, used to 'chandeliers burning, candelabra tall as trees, reliquaries on the altar encrusted with precious stones, mosaic floors, billowing incense and silken altar-cloths, all this under the vaults of a choir so lofty it made him dizzy, in a venerable abbey church filled with images of the saints, echoing with ancient chant under the enormous figure of Christ in majesty dominating the stately apse', was convinced that he lived in an image of the celestial Jerusalem.

On entering a Cistercian church he would have been struck by the meanness of height of the nave, the low, square-ended presbytery, the rough wooden choir stalls, the interior divided up into forbiddingly enclosed sections where not even royalty could trespass. He would have noticed the lack of tombs, the absence of images and lights other than the natural light of day let in through the small windows. A simple wooden cross with a roughly painted image of Christ hanging above the altar was all that reminded him he was in a place of worship. The priest saying Mass wore a chasuble of undyed wool, the deacon and sub-deacon nothing that could identify them as such. The altar, alone in the small squat east end of the church, was covered with a simple white cloth and bore two unadorned iron candlesticks. Nor would our Cluniac recognize the strange, clipped chanting which echoed through this barn of a church. Stephen Harding, in his rejection of Cluniac liturgical excess, remembered the references St Benedict makes in his rule to the hymns of St Ambrose, and once more followed Benedict to the letter. After much study and research, he came up with what he believed to be the original chants of St Ambrose both in word and tune, and had them adopted as part of the standard Cistercian liturgy.

When mention is made of Cistercian architecture, an image is usually conjured up of a style that is obviously not Romanesque and yet would be hard to define as Gothic. In effect, albeit unintentionally, the Cistercians managed to develop a distinct architectural style of their own which, by its very originality, defies inclusion among the traditional denominations. Borrowing the stylistic vocabulary prevalent in Burgundy at the time, the pointed arch, ribbed vaulting and other elements of early Gothic

OPPOSITE ABOVE Le Tre Fontane, Italy. Chancel: typical square-ended chancel, built during St Bernard's lifetime

OPPOSITE BELOW Heisterbach, Germany. Chancel

Silvacane, France. View across nave to south aisle

Clairmont, France. East end: Cistercian architecture at its bleakest

grafted onto a Romanesque interpretation of mass, volume and spatial definition, the Cistercians sought essentially to translate into architecture the principle of perfect measure expressed in geometrically determined harmony of proportion. This principle had first been given currency in the *De Musica* of St Augustine, one of St Bernard's most consistent sources of inspiration.

After the death of Stephen Harding in 1134, the General Chapter implicitly sanctioned official adoption of the style by condemning departure from the austerity and simplicity which were the hallmark of the Order and, over the next hundred years, we find the Chapter reiterating this principle again and again. If the Chapter felt the need to restate its policy continually, we can only assume that it had to combat a natural tendency towards decoration and embellishment. In the course of time it became, not surprisingly, impossible to maintain the spiritual tension and initial burning enthusiasm which had informed the ideals of the founding fathers. What is perhaps more surprising is that the style of building born of that spiritual tension was adhered to for so long. The spate of rebuilding, especially of the east end of churches, which took place after 1153 with Bernard still warm in his grave, sometimes evokes an image of monks straining at the bit under his iron rule, and adhering forcibly to a style they intrinsically disliked, only to replace it without even waiting a decent interval after his death, with something more akin to their natural preferences. This simplistic view fails to take into account, as Bernard himself failed to take into account, the need for expansion due to the sheer number of vocations. Bernard strongly resisted the move to a more convenient site when his own abbey of Clairvaux was patently insufficient to accommodate the growing number of aspiring novices, even though the move only involved a few hundred yards. Similarly, the tendency in many of the major abbey churches, including Cîteaux, Clairvaux, Pontigny and Morimond, to rebuild the small squat east end, and at times the entire church, should be seen not so much as a move away from the canons of austerity typified by what is known at the Bernardine plan, but rather as a realistic attempt to cope with the expanding number of choir monks and an ever-increasing proportion of ordained priests among them.[1] It is significant that amost all the east ends rebuilt in the twelfth and thirteenth centuries were designed to accommodate large numbers of altars, to enable those priests to fulfil their obligation to celebrate Mass daily.

OPPOSITE Le Thoronet, France. Nave

Fontenay, France. West door

RIGHT Fontenay, France. Nave and north aisle

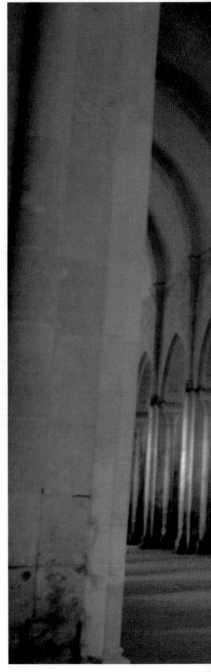

The Cistercian abbey church kept to the standard Benedictine plan in
the use of the Latin cross shape, replacing the rounded apse of Benedictine
tradition and rounded ambulatory with apsidal chapels of more recent
Cluniac inspiration, with a small square-ended chancel. Even when this
small chancel was demolished, it is very rare to see it replaced by one of
the existing traditional east-end types. In many cases a large square chancel would be built with individual chapels all around it, and even when
the new chancel was rounded and took an ambulatory, the chapels leading off it tended to have square end walls. The search for geometric
harmony and consistency was always the inspiring principle.

In the two arms of the Latin cross, the transepts, we find two or three
small private chapels against the east wall on either side of the presbytery,
for ordained monks to say Mass privately. One of the most prominent
features, usually of the south transept, is the night stair. This led directly
from the monks' dormitory into the church and was used by the brethren
to attend the services which took place in the early hours of the morning.
In some cases, where the lie of the land had made it impossible to build
the cloister, and consequently all the conventual buildings, on the south
side of the abbey church, the night stair will be found in the north transept.

At the crossing of the transept arms with the main body of the church,
normally under some form of *tiburium* (crossing tower) which housed the
two bells permitted by the rule, we find the monks' choir. External bell
towers and splendid peals were regarded as typical symbols of Cluniac
pride and expressly forbidden. A maximum of two bells might be housed
in the church and these would normally be placed directly above the choir
with the ropes hanging down over the plain wooden stalls to enable a
monk to ring them when required during the service.

It is often noticeable when wandering around either a Cistercian ruin
or a church which, though intact, has had its furniture moved around, that
the lower part of the pillars or columns of the first few bays of the nave
west of the crossing are left rough and unfinished on the inside. This is
easily explained when one realizes that, since the choir occupied these few
bays (and not the chancel as is often supposed), the stonework would have
been hidden from view by the now vanished wooden stalls. Any finishing
not structurally necessary was therefore superfluous.

OPPOSITE Huerta, Spain. Night stairs: it was down these stairs that the monks
processed directly from bed to choir stall to attend the night-time services

LEFT Vallbona de les Monjes, Spain. Tiburium at the base of the crossing tower

BELOW Riddagshausen, Germany. Chancel chapels from crossing

OPPOSITE Maulbronn, Germany. West door

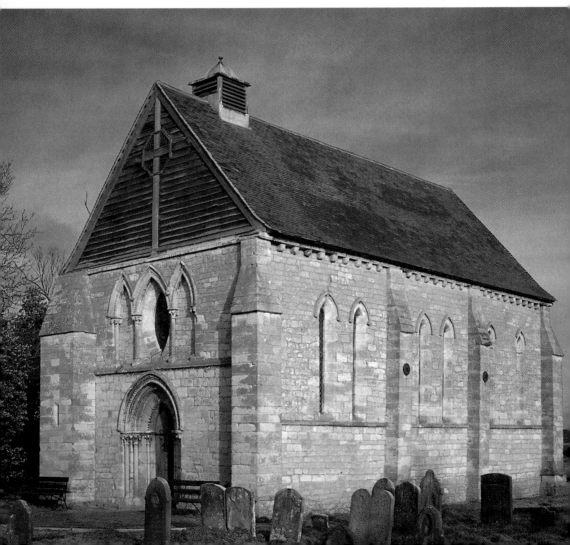

Just beyond the choir, stone or more often wooden benches for the sick and infirm brethren were placed against the stone screen wall which separated the monks' precinct from that of the lay brothers within the church. The lay brothers, whose liturgical obligations were confined to two church attendances a day, had two altars set against the back of the screen. Their stalls occupied the next few bays of the nave, after which came the benches for the elderly and infirm, situated directly against the inside wall of the west front. Since the very essence of a Cistercian abbey church was to interpret the *paradisus claustralis* (cloistered paradise) of a contemplative monastery, no provision was made for a congregation in whose face the doors of the church (and many Cistercian west fronts were indeed without doors) remained rigourously closed. Given the total isolation of the majority of Cistercian settings, this caused few difficulties, and the Cistercians were rarely afflicted by any of the wrangling and bickering that many other orders encountered in their dealings with their 'parishioners'. Passing pilgrims and travellers were catered for in the *capella ad portas* (the chapel at the gates), many fine examples of which survive. Cistercian in style, they make numerous concessions to the decorative fashions of the day, since they were intended for lay visitors to whom the rules of austerity were never meant to apply.

Stephen Harding had in fact created one of the most successful and original schools of manuscript illumination at Cîteaux, and Bernard himself, far from showing insensitivity towards artistic beauty, admits that it is the very attraction of art which made it a potential distraction for his monks from the ideals of contemplative worship: 'All around is such a fantastic variety of figures that it would be easy to prefer fulfiling the *Lectio Divina* (Spiritual Reading) by contemplation of the walls (in church, and the fantastically sculptured capitals in the cloister) rather than by reading a book. It is easier to spend a whole day in ecstatic admiration of these things than in contemplating the law of God'. That Bernard never took any public stance on manuscript illumination in particular may simply show that he wished to avoid being seen to hold a different, more stringent view on the matter than Stephen Harding, thus implicitly criticizing his superior.

OPPOSITE ABOVE Badia a Cerreto, Italy. Façade, showing narthex

OPPOSITE BELOW Kirkstead, England. Chapel at the gates

OVERLEAF San Galgano, Italy. Nave: unfinished stonework on nave pilasters would originally have been hidden by choir stalls

Outside the west front many churches sported some form of portico or narthex, whose purpose is not immediately apparent. Certainly the elaborate narthexes of Cluniac and Benedictine tradition, supposedly built to offer shelter to pilgrims, are the direct derivation of the imposing *westwerk* so characteristic of Carolingian architecture in the eighth and ninth centuries. It seems likely that a portico was accepted as an intrinsic part of monastic church architecture and played some role in ceremonial and processional activities (such as the lighting of the paschal candle at midnight Mass on Easter Saturday); the Cistercians once again simply sheared away the excess and reduced the portico to its most elemental form.

Apart from the main doorway or doorways in the west front, there were five other doors in the abbey church. One was located at the west end of the south aisle and led either directly into the lay brothers' wing or, more likely, a narrow passageway known as the *ruelle des convers* (lay brothers' alley). It was through this door that the lay brothers entered and left the church twice a day. To reach it from the complex of halls and rooms which made up their wing, they would use the narrow *ruelle* which ran parallel to the west walk of the cloister but was completely walled off from it, to ensure that there was minimum contact between the choir monks, usually of noble stock, and the illiterate lay brothers of humbler origin.

The door leading out of the north transept invariably gave onto the monks' cemetery, and is normally known as the lychgate or *porte des morts*. The monks were buried in nameless graves, clad in their habits and laid straight into the ground. They made their last journey through this door, and at all times other than during a funeral service it was kept shut.

At the east end of the south aisle, just before the corner leading round into the south transept, was the choir monks' entrance to the church. This was the door used by the monks to reach their stalls for the daytime services. During the night, as we have seen, they entered the church via the south transept. In many ruins, or in some churches which have been

OPPOSITE ABOVE Valle Crucis, Wales. South transept: dormitory doorway gives onto thin air where night stairs have disappeared

OPPOSITE BELOW Bonnefontaine, France. Collation seat: unique example of a collation seat surviving when the entire south wall of the church and surrounding north cloister walk have gone

OVERLEAF Chiaravalle della Colomba, Italy. Cloister, north-east corner

converted for parochial use and detached from their secularized conventual buildings, the night stair is frequently the first thing to have been demolished, which explains the puzzling presence of a door halfway up a wall and apparently giving out onto thin air.

The last door in the church led out of the south transept at ground level, and can normally be found immediately below the night-stair door. It communicated with the sacristy. Cistercian sacristies are usually much humbler in proportion and scale than those in the churches of other less austere orders, since the monks vested directly at the altar, and yet even in these secondary spaces we find the love of geometric clarity and harmony which manages to weld the vast and disparate buildings of the conventual complex into such a satisfying unitary whole.

If we leave the church by the monks' daytime doorway, we immediately find ourselves in the north walk of the cloister. The cloister, a gallery comprising four walks and a central garth, is the true centre of monastic daily life, just as the church is the centre of the monks' spiritual life. Originally derived from the Roman *atrium*, a central courtyard off which opened all the main rooms of the house, the cloister serves the same basic purpose in the monastery. All the main functions of monastic life take place in rooms or buildings which give onto the cloister, and to get from any one part of the monastery to another one must cross this space. It is in fact a masterpiece of functional planning, raised to new heights of spatial dignity by the simplicity of Cistercian design. Situated wherever possible on the south side of the church, to take full advantage of natural sunlight, the cloister was frequently a simple, wooden lean-to structure only replaced in stone when every other building in the monastery had been completed. The arcading could vary from tight spaces with walling in between, especially in the hot south where it served as protection against the merciless midday sun, to wide arches carried on slender columns to let in as much sunshine as possible, and even, in the far north, to glazing in order to afford some measure of shelter against the freezing winters of Scotland and Scandinavia.

While the cloister was basically a service area, it also performed a number of functions in its own right. On the cloister side of the south wall of the church there stood the collation seat, with benches on either side of it, where the abbot would sit after supper, surrounded by his flock, while a monk read to them from the Bible, the Lives of the Saints or other edifying literature.

OPPOSITE La Oliva, Spain. Cloister, north walk

The Cistercians, at least in the intentions of the founders, were not an intellectual order, and the books an abbey was allowed to keep were few. This becomes evident when we note the size of the *armarium* or book cupboard, situated in the east wall of the cloister, just by the monks' doorway and next to or in front of the sacristy. In very few cases could it contain more than forty or fifty books of the size usual in the Middle Ages, and frequently they failed to reach that number. The titles permitted were strictly dictated by the Annual General Chapter and normally included works considered indispensable for liturgical purposes, for the *lectio divina* or the *meditatio*, both performed in the cloister, and occasionally included works by the monks themselves.

One of the most beautiful rooms off the east walk of the cloister is invariably the chapterhouse. So called because a chapter from the rule of St Benedict was read to the monks assembled in it, the chapterhouse was usually a square or rectangular room divided into bays with one or more columns in its centre. The typical entrance to the chapterhouse consists of two twin-light windows, one on either side of the arched entrance doorway. The large unglazed windows were designed to enable representatives of the lay brothers to sit in on meetings and hear the abbey business discussed each day after the reading of the chapter and the confession of faults. The monks themselves sat on the stone bench which ran all the way around the wall on the inside, interrupted only by the abbot's seat placed directly opposite the entrance. It was in this room that the abbots were given a slightly more dignified burial than their less exalted brethren were entitled to. Today the floors of many chapterhouses are paved with exquisite tombstones extolling the virtues of one or other of the abbots.

The door next to the chapterhouse gave onto the day stairs leading up to the dormitory which occupied the whole of the upper storey of the east wing. Contrary to popular belief, the monks slept in their habits on

OPPOSITE ABOVE Eberbach, Germany. Dormitory. By the late thirteenth century the spartan appearance of the dormitory had been somewhat mitigated and it was usual for wooden partitions (here long since removed) to separate the palliasses of the individual monks. This dormitory was used as the setting for the scriptorium in the film *The Name of the Rose*

OPPOSITE BELOW Arnsburg, Germany. Cloister, north-east corner: monks' daytime doorway from church to cloister, and book cupboard

OVERLEAF Rueda, Spain. Chapter house, entrance

straw-filled mattresses on the floor in a common room where perhaps only the abbot had a curtain to afford him some little privacy. It was not before the very end of the Middle Ages that the single dormitory, usually an open space vaulted in wood or stone, was divided up into cells by the construction of flimsy partition walls between the beds.

Beyond the dormitory, a separate room housed what is known as the reredorter or latrine block, used by all the brothers immediately after the second service of the morning. The reredorter was normally a hall-like structure divided into cubicles by wooden partitions. Each cubicle contained a horizontal wooden board (the Venetian for 'small board' or 'plank' is *toleta*, from which the word 'toilet' is indirectly derived) pierced by two holes (the monks used the 'toilets' two to a cubicle) giving directly onto the fast-flowing stream below. Anyone who has visited a Cistercian monastery cannot fail to be aware of the immense importance the architects attached to the system of drains and plumbing in general. A glance at the standard plan of a monastery, or a visit to Fountains or Netley, Eberbach or Maulbronn, Fontenay or Fontaine-Guérard will confirm the complexity and innovation of Cistercian sanitary engineering. The brook which was always a key element of a Cistercian site was diverted upstream of the reredorter, so that while the main current flowed directly under the latrine cubicles in a stone-lined channel, a branch tunnelled under the dormitory, emerging in the cloister in the form of a washing fountain, continuing its journey via the kitchens and rejoining the main brook thereafter.

St Bernard's first biographer describes how the monks building the abbey of Clairvaux 'divided the river, set it in new channels and lifted the leaping waters to the mill-wheels; fullers and bakers and tanners and smiths and other artificers prepared suitable machines for their tasks, that the river might flow fast and do good wherever it was needed in every building, flowing freely in the underground conduits; the streams performed suitable tasks in every office and cleansed the abbey and at length returned to the main course what it had lost'. The forge at Fontenay is a

OPPOSITE ABOVE Bebenhausen, Germany. Dormitory. By the fifteenth century each monk had his own cell

OPPOSITE BELOW Bebenhausen, Germany. Monks' dayroom, capital

OVERLEAF Noirlac, France. Chapter house window

wonderful example of what the writer is describing, where the thundering of the water seems to invade every nook and cranny, and one can still almost feel the monks sweating and toiling over their work in one of Europe's first industrial buildings.

Below the dormitory is usually situated one of the rooms whose exact purpose and function is a matter of controversy. Diversely described in guide books and pamphlets as the '*scriptorium*', the 'monks' day-room', the 'novices' room' and even the 'refectory' or 'novices' refectory', no one seems to be quite sure what this room was for, for the simple reason that St Bernard makes no mention of it. The most logical explanation for its existence seems to lie in the need, as numbers swelled, to enlarge the dormitory overhead. Since the dormitory could no longer be contained in the space available over the sacristy, chapterhouse and day stairs, a new ground-floor room automatically came into being. Usually a vaulted room with a row of pillars down the centre dividing it into two aisles, the monks' room rarely opened directly onto the cloister. Instead it gave onto a passageway leading to the area behind the east range, occupied more often than not by the infirmary and connected buildings or the herb and vegetable garden. Sometimes this passageway was adjacent to or acted as the 'parlour', the only space in the monastic enclosure where the monks were allowed to talk. The vow of silence was so strict that even then the parlour was used mostly for the prior to impart his instructions concerning the work rota to the monks after chapter rather than for any idle chatter between the brethren.

The south walk of the cloister, furthest removed from the church, gave access to a series of rooms concerned principally with relieving, to a small extent, the rigours of an ascetic life. The first room housed the *calefactorium* or warming-house, the only room in the entire monastery apart from the kitchen where a fire was allowed, and even then the fire was lit only when the holy water in the stoup in the abbey church had frozen over! The warming-house was strategically placed next to the monks' day-room to take the edge off the frozen air that would have made much of their written work impossible to execute. Even then, it is recorded that at Kirkstall in northern England, the brothers stuffed their stockings with hay to stop their toes freezing during the winter months. It was also in this room that the monks had their hair tonsured and their beards cut seven times a year.

OPPOSITE Noirlac, France. Refectory

Maulbronn, Germany. Refectory

Maulbronn, Germany. Wash house: half-timbered upper floor added later

Le Thoronet, France. Cloister, east walk

OPPOSITE ABOVE Noirlac, France. Cloister, north walk
OPPOSITE BELOW L'Epau, France. Chapter house

The dominant feature of the south walk of the cloister is the *lavatorium* or wash-house, a generally octagonal pagoda in Cistercian abbeys, built out into the cloister garth midway down the arcade and housing a one- or two- or sometimes even three-tiered fountain at which the monks washed their hands and heads before meals. It lies directly across the cloister walk from the entrance to the refectory. In view of the exquisite beauty of the examples extant, it is a great shame that this more than any other building, perhaps because of its fragility, has totally disappeared from the majority of Cistercian abbeys, whether in ruin or still in use. Sometimes the pagoda was replaced by a simple trough placed against the south wall of the cloister and surmounted by a bench on which the monks could sit with their feet in the water for the *mandatum* ceremony, the washing of the feet.

Refectories are in themselves among the most imposing of the buildings to be seen in a Cistercian monastery. Unlike the majority of monastic orders, from about the mid-twelfth century onward, the Cistercians almost always built their refectories perpendicular rather than parallel to the south walk of the cloister. Where they failed to do so after that date, the lie of the land, lack of funds or the presence of a pre-existing building normally account for the anomaly. Many words have been spent in attempting to explain why the Cistercians should have adopted this peculiar difference as one of their hallmarks. Nothing is known of the position of the original refectory at Cîteaux before the arrival of St Bernard and his companions. It may still have been of wood. What is certain, however, is that Bernard's mother, Lady Aleth, had been buried in the Abbey of St Bénigne in Dijon, an abbey Bernard and his family knew well and visited frequently, given their devotion to that saintly lady. The refectory of St Bénigne, uniquely for a Benedictine abbey, is set perpendicular to the cloister. Scholars of the eminence of Professor Braunfels feel that this can be no mere coincidence. Another perhaps more persuasive reason has recently been put forward by Peter Fergusson. Professor Fergusson maintains that the repositioning of the refectory 'was

OPPOSITE ABOVE Huerta, Spain. Refectory: on the left of the picture can clearly be seen the reader's pulpit

OPPOSITE BELOW Reigny, France. Refectory: currently houses a fine collection of old cars and carriages

Roche, England. Plumbing. The reduction of the conventual buildings at Roche to little more than their foundations provides an excellent opportunity to appreciate the ingenuity of Cistercian plumbing. This picture was taken from the site of the kitchen yard. From here the stream passed under the foundations of the refectory (first 'bridge'), past the monks' room (second 'bridge') and out through the reredorter (latrine) to pursue its course back into nature, taking with it all the biodegradable waste the monastery needed to dispose of

OPPOSITE Valle Crucis, Wales. Chapter house.

part of a complete reorganization of the south side of the cloister'. The refectory was realigned as a consequence of the need to render directly accessible from the cloister two rooms, the warming house and the kitchen, which had hitherto (in Benedictine and early Cistercian monasteries) lain outside the cloister. In Professor Fergusson's words:

> it was the position of these two structures ... which presented the Cistercians with a trying conflict. Strict adherence to the rule of St Benedict *ad litteram* lay at the heart of the Cistercian reform. Thus monks took turns to serve as cooks week by week. Yet in the traditional layout, kitchen and warming house were inaccessible from the cloister and thus cooking and warming could be accomplished only by infringing the rule.

By realigning the refectory so that its narrow side abutted the south cloister walk, the kitchen and warming-house could be brought in to occupy the space freed up by the move, enabling direct access from the cloister. The problem was thus solved. Professor Fergusson claims there is some evidence that Clairvaux was the first abbey to adopt this plan, some time around 1150, three years before St Bernard died. Is it too fanciful to suggest that it was while seeking a solution to this infringement of the rule, that St Bernard's memory went back to the abbey where his mother was buried and there found his answer?

Whatever the origin of the realignment, this positioning of the refectory enabled the designers and architects of the monasteries to express some of their most inspiring work. A lofty two-storey great hall, generally vaulted and divided into two aisles by a row of pillars, it had nothing to hinder the construction of a row of tall windows down either side of its length, to allow the light to come flooding in all day long. A constant feature of the refectory is the *pulpitum* or reader's pulpit, from which one of the brethren would read aloud during mealtimes from the Bible, the Lives of the Saints, the Rule of St Benedict and so forth. In contemplating these magnificent structures, it is interesting to ponder the words of Peter Cantor, a monk of Longpont, who says that St Bernard would burst into tears every time he passed the wretched thatch and timber or wattle and daub huts of the peasants, because he was 'reminded of the early days of the Cistercians'.

Immediately adjacent to the refectory is the kitchen, served by running water from the brook channelled beneath its floor. Occasionally the water would flow directly into a small pool inside the kitchen and escape through an overflow, but only after first depositing any fish swimming in it as prisoners in the pool! This exceptional arrangement can still be seen at the Abbey of Alcobaça in Portugal. It was more usual, however, for the monks to have their own *vivarium* or fish pond in the grounds. The kitchen sometimes had a serving hatch on either side of it, one side communicating with the monks' refectory, the other giving onto the lay brothers' building.

The entire west range, normally separated from the cloister proper by the *ruelle des convers* (lay brothers' alley), was devoted to the lay brothers and their activities and responsibilities. The arrangement of the buildings was similar to that on the monks' side of the cloister, with a large refectory situated on the ground floor adjacent to the kitchen. It usually rose only one storey in height, with the dormitory extending the full length of the west range over it.

Underneath the dormitory, to the north, lay the *cellarium* or storehouse, another room similar in construction to the lay brothers' refectory, with a single row of pillars down the middle to divide it into a two-aisled vaulted space. Between the *cellarium* and the lay brothers' refectory stood the main gateway into the monastic enclosure, usually no more than a tunnel leading past the *ruelle des convers* into the south-west corner of the cloister. Many of the lay brothers' buildings, after falling into disuse with the demise of the 'conversus' system,[2] were converted into comfortable private apartments by the abbot for his own use and the entertaining of guests.

Without doubt the most important subsidiary building in the abbey grounds was the infirmary. Cistercian asceticism was a regime that not everyone was able to tolerate with the same degree of physical resistance, and the old and infirm accounted for a fair proportion of any monastery's population. Most infirmaries were originally not unlike the refectory building in design, two-storey in height with one or two rows of columns down the middle to divide them into aisles. Beds, one per bay, were sometimes screened off from each other by curtains but it was not until the fifteenth century that the first cubicles appeared. The beds were lined up perpendicular to the side walls so that their occupants could get a good view of the altar containing the blessed sacrament which stood against the end wall. In later times, a separate chapel would be built, and a separate kitchen, known as the meat kitchen, to provide slightly more substantial

LEFT Longpont, France.
Warming house

BELOW Mariental, Germany.
Lay brothers' refectory

OPPOSITE Sénanque, France.
Lay brothers' dormitory

meals for the sick than the rule permitted for the hale. Eventually all these buildings were, quite naturally, grouped around a small cloister, with a herb garden often occupying the garth. A splendid example of this arrangement can be seen at Eberbach in the Rhineland, although the buildings now house a wine cellar and, apart from a small area used for wine tasting, are not generally open to the public.

Numerous other outbuildings occupied much of the ground between the monastic enclosure proper and the wall running round the abbey land. These might include industrial buildings such as the forge already mentioned, or mills, pigeon-coops or dovecotes, workshops, the bakery or, as at Villers-la-Ville in Brabant, a brewery of industrial proportions. They would undoubtedly have included, at least from the thirteenth century on, some form of guest accommodation, and in some cases a market hall, fine examples of which can be seen at Staffarda in the Piedmont. The gate-house itself could often be of quite some size and occasionally house the guest lodgings, pharmacy, herbarium or other functions. The *capella ad portas*, or strangers' chapel, for non-monastic worship, was generally situated just outside the gatehouse.

In their determination to be totally self-supporting, the Cistercians refused in principle to accept the tithes and dues which had enabled abbeys such as Cluny to accrue great wealth. Over the years this rule was increasingly relaxed, to the point of making the order virtually indistinguishable from any other in this regard. By the time of the Black Death in 1348 the lay brother work force was so decimated that strict observance of this precept was no longer a viable proposition. (The first recorded instance of a Cistercian abbey agreeing to own a property simply for the revenue it would bring in goes back to 1189, when Richard the Lionheart gave Scarborough parish church to the abbey of Rievaulx, also in Yorkshire.) The vast properties which they acquired through donations and endowments required skilled management. It was thanks to the need to institutionalize the figure of the lay brother and the grange system to provide this management that the Cistercian order made its outstanding contribution to the development of agriculture in Europe. Much of the old Continent's agricultural layout today owes its appearance to the order.

OPPOSITE Bon-Repos, France. Gatehouse

OVERLEAF Fountains, England. By the late fifteenth century statutes prohibiting sumptuous bell towers were largely ignored

In Burgundy and on the Rhine, the monks perfected the art of viticulture, producing many of the finest wines in these areas on estates still renowned for the quality of their vintages. Meursault and the Clos Vougeot, Steinberg with its famous Riesling and Nierstein on the Rhine are but some of the world-famous vineyards which began life in the care of the white monks. The abbey of Himmerod owned many of the most prosperous wine-growing areas along the banks of the Moselle, and it is no surprise to learn that, all in all, the sale of wine was the order's single most profitable enterprise.

In England and Wales, the Cistercians were the largest body of sheep farmers in the country, their yield playing a major role in Britain's export trade in the twelfth and thirteenth centuries, supplying wool for the looms of Flanders and Italy. Their granges, with the vast barns sometimes called tithe barns (erroneously since the order refused tithes), were the single most effective agrarian institution of the Middle Ages. When King Richard the Lionheart was held in captivity in Germany in 1193, the Cistercians repaid his generosity of four years before and emptied their barns to the tune of one whole year's yield of wool as a contribution to the ransom, and the Cistercian abbots of Boxley and Robertsbridge were entrusted with negotiating Richard's release.

The lay brothers also ran the markets for which many abbeys were granted charters, and worked the flour mills which played an important part in bolstering abbey revenues. With their specialist knowledge of draining and irrigation, acquired in turning marshy bogs into 'clear valleys', they became experts in pisciculture. Some abbeys even appointed a *frater piscatorius* to manage the fish ponds and look after the wholesale of their produce. The Abbey of Waldsassen in Germany had over 150 fish tanks supplying fresh carp and trout to the whole of the Upper Palatinate.

The Cistercians' fruit orchards were famous throughout Germany, and in Belgium their beer is still considered to be the best brewed today. The building reputed to be a vast brewery at the Abbey of Villers-la-Ville near

OPPOSITE ABOVE Tilty, England. Chapel at the gates: modern whitewash covers original decorative scheme

OPPOSITE BELOW Fontenay, France. Forge

OVERLEAF Fountains, England. Lay brothers' wing: originally partitioned into separate areas (refectory, cellarium etc.)

Brussels bears eloquent witness to this profitable activity even in its ruined state. The order's insistence on uniformity in all things, including diet, probably accounted for the invention by the brothers in the cooler northern climes of their most lasting contribution to horticulture: the greenhouse.

The lay brothers were also unwitting actors in Europe's first industrial revolution after the fall of the Roman Empire. The British Isles provided the setting for the Cistercians' pioneering work in the fields of coal mining, at Newbattle and Culross abbeys in Scotland, and at Neath, Margam and Llantarnam in Wales, lead mining and foundry work at Fountains, Basingwerk, Strata Florida and Strata Marcella, and the mining and smelting of iron ore at Furness, Flaxley, Rievaulx, Kirkstall, Jervaulx, Byland, Sawley, Louth Park and Stanley in England, Grace-Dieu, Tintern and Margam in Wales. Masters of metallurgy, the Cistercians invented the camshaft to exploit hydraulic energy to drive the machinery and bellows in their forges. The Abbey of San Tommaso dei Borgognoni on the island of Torcello in the Venetian lagoon was heated by natural gas. A document recently found hidden in a bottle concealed in the chimney in the one surviving wall of the gatehouse recounts how a brother was killed in the late sixteenth century when a gas leakage caused an explosion and the ceiling of the porter's room fell on his head.

In France, the abbeys of Fontenay, La Crête, Clairvaux, Igny and Trois-Fontaines were all famed for their ironworks, while Walkenreid in Germany and its daughter-house Sittichenbach specialized in copper mining. Another daughter–house of Walkenreid, called Grünhain, mined coal and iron and silver, as did the abbeys of Altzelle in Saxony, and Ossegg and Sedletz in Bohemia. The Abbey of Rein, the first Cistercian foundation in Austria, possessed the largest salt mine in the area, and in northern Germany the salt pits of Magdeburg, Marlow and Lüneburg were exploited by the Cistercians from neighbouring abbeys. Doberan and Reinfeld owed their prosperity to this activity, as did the Abbey of Wąchock near Cracow in Poland. The production of salt in an age where the absence of refrigeration meant that most food had to be salted down for the winter, was obviously of vital importance in all areas of Europe and played a major role in the economies of the abbeys of Holmcultram, Calder, Furness, Byland, Newminster, Jervaulx and Louth Park in England, Quarr on the Isle of Wight and Clairvaux in Champagne.

4. The Monks, the Monastery and the Monastic Day

UT WHAT OF THE MONKS and lay brothers who peopled the abbeys? How was their day organized? First of all we should remember that until reasonably accurate clocks were introduced in the seventeenth century, the monks' day, like that of most of the rest of Christendom, depended on the sun and was thus subject to considerable variation according to the seasons. The difference, of course, was that most of the rest of Christendom went to bed at dusk and got up just after dawn. The monks spent half the night in church.

Once a novice had been through a year's novitiate, he would be accepted into the community as a fully-fledged choir monk. Rising from his palliasse on the cold floor of the dormitory at about 1.30 a.m., already clad in his habit, he joined his brethren in the aisle between the rows of mattresses and together they processed towards the door which led down the night stairs and into the choir stalls. The service of matins lasted for an hour, followed after a short interval by lauds. In winter this interval lasted four and a half hours, giving the monks time to return to the dormitory for a rest until 7 a.m. In summer, prime followed lauds at 4 a.m., and was in turn followed at sunrise by private mass and the conventual morning mass. In winter this sequence was inverted and prime took place at 8 a.m. after the morning mass.

The first appointment of the day outside the church was chapter. Held at 4.30 a.m. in the summer, chapter only started after tierce at about 9.30 a.m. in the winter. During chapter the abbot or prior, whichever of the two was conducting the ceremony, read out and commented on the relevance of a chapter from the Rule of St Benedict, after which the monks were encouraged to confess their sins or others' sins known to them in front of their brethren and to invite chastisement for the sake of charity. Only by helping each other lovingly to mend their ways could they do justice to the spirit of charity on which the whole philosophical design of Cîteaux rested.

This was followed by a discussion of any business the abbey might have that day, and on Sundays and holy days a reading was taken from the *Book of Usages* and the *Statutes of the General Chapter* of the order. Chapter was also the setting for the acceptance of novices, the vestition of new monks, the profession of the vows, and the naming of officials to their new posts, such as cellarer, novice master and prior. Chapter ended with a commemoration of the brothers who had passed on to eternal life, and the recital of the *De Profundis*.

As the brethren filed out of the chapterhouse, the vaulted parlour already echoed to the sound of Brother Prior beating a stick on the wooden *tabula* or sounding board, calling them together for the allocation of their daily tasks. Each monk would then return up the day stairs to the dormitory, collect his tools from beside his mattress and silently make his way to his place of work, be it the herb garden, the fields, the forge or the dovecote, the sheep-pen or the *scriptorium*.

A bell, or in the more austere monasteries a wooden clapper, called the monks to the service of sext at about 11 a.m., which brought the morning to a close. In summer, sext was followed immediately by lunch in the refectory. Before entering the hall, all the brethren crowded into the washhouse opposite the refectory door and washed their hands and heads to remove all trace of ink, mud and dust. This was the only occasion in the whole day when the monks washed, although it is not unreasonable to suppose that the washing of the feet, or *mandatum*,[^1] which took place every Saturday evening from Easter to 14 September served a practical as well as a ceremonial purpose. Whatever the case, its importance is underlined by St Bernard's proposal to make it the eighth sacrament. Concepts of personal hygiene in the Middle Ages were of course very different to those of today, and what is remarkable is not that the monks by our standards washed so little, but rather that such strict insistence was laid on washing heads and hands daily. Taking a bath was another matter. Regarded as a

OPPOSITE ABOVE Le Tre Fontane, Italy. Chapter house, with recycled classical columns and capitals

OPPOSITE BELOW Eberbach, Germany. Chapter house. The monks would have sat on the stone benches clearly visible around the base of the walls

sensual luxury, incompatible with St Bernard's injunction to those who entered Cîteaux to 'leave their bodies at the gate', bathing was permitted in the infirmary alone. Anyone leaving the abbey precinct to go in search of a hot bath was not allowed back into the monastery.

We know of at least three separate occasions at which monks earned themselves a severe reprimand for taking a bath. The natural sulphur springs of Etruria proved too great a temptation for the Abbot of San Giusto di Tuscania, who was admonished by the General Chapter of 1202 for picnicking with laymen and then removing his habit to bathe in the springs outside the abbey grounds. A monk of Hautecombe in Savoie was required to explain his behaviour in eating meat and bathing in 1212, and the Abbot of Pilis in Hungary in 1225 had dared to go to the public baths on Holy Saturday and be given a shave. It is only towards the middle of the fifteenth century that baths began to be considered a necessity rather than a luxury, reflecting the evolution of general social standards. Even then, however, a bath once a month was deemed perfectly sufficient, with the specific proviso that it be taken in silence and not become an occasion for rowdy and unseemly behaviour.

Lunch in the refectory never lasted more than about half an hour, and was taken in silence. As the brothers ate their frugal meal, one of them read to the community from the Bible and the writings of the Church Fathers. Those who finished first were encouraged to form a cross with the stray breadcrumbs on the table in front of them as they listened to the readings, to prevent their minds from wandering. During the centuries of strict adherence to the rule, everything the monks ate was produced by the abbey, a tangible demonstration of its aspirations to self-sufficiency. At their two meals a day in the summer, or their one daily repast in the winter, the brethren were allowed an abundance of bread and vegetables, flavoured with herbs from their garden, fish and eggs on feast days, occasionally cheese, and about three-quarters of a litre of wine, or beer and cider in colder northern climes. But under absolutely no circumstances, outside the infirmary, was meat ever present on the table. In the words of St Bernard: 'I abstain from meat because if I feed my body too much, I nourish carnal desire thereby; I eat bread in moderation, because a heavy stomach prevents me from standing up straight at my prayers'. To guard against the temptations of the flesh, the monks were also subjected to blood-letting four times a year, and meat was only permitted in the infirmary on the premise that its inhabitants were already well out of

Satan's grasp, either too old or too ill to spare the pleasures of the flesh more than a passing thought.

Lunch ended with grace said by the prior, and an act of thanksgiving in the abbey church. After this service, or immediately after lunch on Fridays during Lent, when all the brothers were allowed was bread and water, there followed a welcome siesta (the very word deriving from sext, the service preceding lunch) of one or two hours, and then back to the choir stalls for nones. In winter, lunch followed rather than preceded nones since it was the only meal of the day.

A few hours' work occupied the afternoon, until vespers was rung at 6 p.m. At supper, immediately after vespers in summer, vegetables and fruit accompanied the remainders of each monk's loaf from lunch. After supper the monks gathered in the north walk of the cloister to hear a reading, the 'collation', given by one of the brothers. The abbot sat against the south wall of the church, the reader opposite him and the monks in a row on the cold stone benches of the cloister arcading.

Following collation, the final service of the day, compline, took place at about 7.30 p.m. and by 8 p.m. the brethren were asleep on their mattresses, wrapped in their habits with a single rough blanket pulled over them. They managed to snatch almost six hours' sleep (in winter, with no supper served, vespers was held at 3.30 p.m., compline at 4 p.m., and with the light failing, the monks took themselves to the dormitory and slept a full nine hours) before the bell for matins woke them again at 1.30 a.m.

When one of the brothers had come to the end of his earthly voyage, his brethren gathered around him to witness the administration of extreme unction, laying him on a mattress over a layer of ashes on the floor. After death, the body was placed on a stone table, stripped and washed. Though the story may be apocryphal, it was apparently only during this ceremony that the brothers of the Abbey of Schönau realized that they had had a sister in their midst for some years. The 'blessed Hildegund' had gone on a pilgrimage to the Holy Land with her father, but he died leaving her alone in a foreign land. Eventually she made her way back to Germany and was admitted to Schönau by the abbot who was convinced that she was a young boy. Realizing her good fortune in a world full of uncertainty for a girl in her position, without a dowry to enter a convent, she kept up this pretence until her death in 1188.

The dead brother was clothed in the full habit, his corpse watched over for the rest of the day and the following night by his erstwhile brethren, then a requiem mass was offered in his memory, and the brothers finally accompanied him through the small door in the north transept of the abbey church to the grave awaiting him. Many monasteries kept a grave permanently dug in readiness for the next occupant; as soon as it was filled, another was dug. The monk was lowered into the cold earth without coffin or shroud, to rest for ever in a nameless unmarked grave. No wooden cross nor coffin could be needed by a brother who had left his body at the gate many years before.

5. From St Bernard to the French Revolution

The great tree of Cîteaux grew prodigiously: in less than a century, its branches stretched out to the frontiers of Christianity, from Alvastra in Sweden and Tuterø in Norway, Mellifont and Boyle in Ireland, to Sambucina in the Calabrian mountains of Sila and Osera in Galicia, Alcobaça in Portugal and Wąchock in Poland. Then, imperceptibly, the branches stop reaching out. The leaves fan out peacefully under the warm sun of the 13th century and the tree confines its activities to producing the season's fruits.

(Van der Meer, F. *Atlas de l'Ordre Cistercien*)

THUS FRÉDÉRIC VAN DER MEER describes the fate of the Cistercian Order after the first great wave of enthusiasm had subsided and the zeal of the founding fathers had been tempered by the practicality of their heirs. The history of the Order after the death of St Bernard is one of limited, if still substantial, expansion, and of consolidation. Cîteaux became part and parcel of the establishment. This is not to say that, within the confines of the monastery, their particular asceticism waned. Throughout the Middle Ages there continued to exist a crucial difference in spirituality between the Cistercians and their rivals the Cluniacs. If anything, the acceptance of the Cistercians by the world at large meant that they themselves still influenced the world to a greater extent than that to which their own ideals were watered down by contact with it.

Many other religious orders during the Middle Ages were inspired by or even copied the practices, architecture and spiritual approach of the Cistercians. The Premonstratensians, the followers of Joachim of Flora, the Franciscans and Dominicans: none would have accomplished what they did without the impact on twelfth century society of the Cistercian revolution.

The history of the Cistercian Order from the death of St Bernard to the eve of the French Revolution, covering a timespan of over 600 years, is remarkable for many reasons, not least for the extent to which members of an order which renounced the world became actively involved in the political vicissitudes of that world.

The careers of two prominent members of the Cistercian Order in the twelfth century highlight the move towards involvement with the world in the latter part of the century. St Ailred of Rievaulx, often referred to as a second St Bernard, spent almost as much time away from his abbey as did St Bernard himself, persuading monarchs to support this or that papal cause, and engaged in other royal business. And yet his whole life, to judge from his writings, is one long hymn to the perfection of Cistercian isolation. It is he who gives us our first glimpse, after Stephen Harding, of the gentler side to the asceticism of Cîteaux. His writings pulse with the pleasure he took in the beauty of his surroundings, however harsh and unwelcoming, and the impression we are left with is of a smile bestowed on those who were the poorer for not sharing the privilege of living in the Cistercian desert.

Baldwin of Forde, on the other hand, a second generation Cistercian, already begins to show many of the signs that were inevitably to weaken Cistercian isolation from the weighty affairs of the world. After strenuously defending Thomas Becket against King Henry II during his youth, he became Bishop of Worcester and then, as Archbishop of Canterbury and Primate of England, he accompanied Henry's son Richard the Lionheart on crusade to the Holy Land.

The third crusade (1189–1192) was preached and to a large extent organized by the order. Gerard, Archbishop of Ravenna, Cistercian monk and papal legate to the Christian armies, Henry of Marcy, Cardinal of Albano and former Abbot of Clairvaux, and Baldwin, Archbishop of Canterbury, were the driving forces behind recruitment for the crusade in Italy, France, England and Germany. All three were to die during the siege of Acre, which saw the triumph of Richard the Lionheart.

When Pope Innocent III, probably the most forceful pope in the history of the Middle Ages in defense of the temporal power of the papacy,

OPPOSITE Daphni, Greece. Cloister arcade

OVERLEAF Vignogoul, France. Chancel vault

wondered who should be sent in the wake of the fourth crusade to the newly conquered Latin Empire of the East to prove the superiority of Roman Christianity over that propounded by the Orthodox Church, the answer could only be the Cistercians. In fact the monks of Cîteaux had again played a major part in organizing the crusade, and Abbot Luca of Sambucina had been entrusted with preaching the cause, soon joined by six other abbots of the order.

When the wily Venetians hijacked the Christian armies, persuading de Villehardouin and his fellow Christian commanders to attack Constantinople ('hive of heretics and schismatics', and incidentally Venice's chief commercial rival in the Mediterranean) abbots Peter of Lucedio and Guy of the Vaux-de-Cernay were among the most outspoken opponents of the Venetian conspiracy and immediately reported it to Innocent III, sadly to no avail. After the sack of Constantinople in 1204, however, the Cistercians, realistic in their acceptance of the situation, wasted no time in colonizing the new Latin Empire, in a well-meaning attempt to show what they believed to be the true path of Christ to the schismatic Orthodox Greeks. In Constantinople itself they took over no less than five monasteries, and on mainland Greece they made three foundations of some importance, one of which was to last until the Turkish conquest of Constantinople in 1453. There are still impressive ruins to be seen at Zaraka in the Peloponnese, and the former Cistercian abbey of Daphni, now returned to the Orthodox Church, is one of the wonders of Attica.

In the Holy Land, during the brief and turbulent existence of the Latin Kingdom of Jerusalem, the Order founded four abbeys and two convents of nuns both dedicated to the Magdalen. The very existence of the Latin Kingdom, however, was fragile and the most important of the male abbeys, Belmont in the Lebanon whose buildings are still miraculously intact and currently occupied by Orthodox monks, saw which way the wind was blowing. Soon after the disastrous battle of the Horns of Hattin in 1187, in which the entire Christian army was decimated by the Moslem forces of Saladin, the monks of Belmont founded the Abbey of Beaulieu near Nicosia in Cyprus. When the crusader kingdom finally fell in 1289, the brethren had a new home ready and waiting for them. Beaulieu was finally demolished in 1567 by the Venetians who needed the stone to shore up the walls of Nicosia against the onslaught of the Turks.

The role played by the Cistercians in the crusade against the Cathars, or Albigensians, heretics who spurned Rome as the living incarnation of

Valle Crucis, Wales. The ruined chancel of the abbey church and the late fifteenth-century prior's chamber reflected in the vivarium, or fish pond the biblical 'Whore of Babylon', is a source of controversy. St Bernard had spent some time in the 1140s preaching orthodoxy in the south west of France among the communities of Cathar followers and had had a reasonable amount of success. It was only natural therefore that Popes Alexander III and, after him, Innocent III, exasperated by these heretics, should call on the Cistercians to supply them with preachers to send among the rebels. Garin of Pontigny and Henry of Clairvaux were the first to take up the challenge, followed by Ranieri of Ponza and Guy of Cîteaux. When Ranieri died, he was replaced by Peter of Castelnau, a monk of the Languedoc Abbey of Fontfroide. Finally, in 1204, the pope placed the task squarely at the feet of Arnaud Amaury, Abbot of Cîteaux.

The first Cistercian missions had been characterized by peaceful attempts at persuasion and dialogue. The debate of Montréal and Pamier in 1207, during which twelve Cistercian abbots led by Amaury and including Guy of the Vaux-de-Cernay discussed doctrinal matters with the *parfaits* (the priests) of the Cathar religion, is the most famous of these episodes and also the last. Peter of Castelnau pleaded the pope for help in his wearying task and was sent two ecclesiastics from Spain: Diego Bishop of Osma and his young assistant Dominic Guzman. They both symbolically donned the Cistercian habit but soon found it too charitable for their liking. They were convinced the rebels could be brought round by something a little stiffer than dialogue.

In 1208, just after the arrival of Dominic Guzman on the scene, the rebels realized that the possibilities offered by peaceful dialogue had come to an end. The murder of Peter of Castelnau sparked off a bloody persecution which lasted over forty years, until the Cathars had virtually ceased to exist as an organized sect. To the eternal shame of the Order, it was the Abbot of Cîteaux Arnaud Amaury who, when asked by the captain of the Catholic army during the sack of Béziers how to distinguish the heretics among the inhabitants who had taken refuge in the church of the Magdalen, is claimed to have said: 'Kill them all! God will recognize his own.' The massacre commenced forthwith.

Whether this famous story is true or a legend, it effectively illustrates how the spirit of violence which was to characterize the Order founded by Dominic Guzman, and the terrifying methods of his Holy Inquisitors, had taken the upper hand over the spirit of charity which governed the Cistercian ideal. The Dominicans, the self-styled Order of Preachers, were soon to become known as the 'Domini Canes', the hounds of the Lord.

And yet after the royal house of France which united the territories of the Counts of Toulouse to the crown, and the papacy that strengthened its spiritual hold in the area, it was not the Dominicans but the Cistercians who reaped the richest pickings of the crusade, with members of the Order becoming bishops of Narbonne, Toulouse and Carcassonne.

Just as the Cistercians had been the inspiration behind the Knights Templar, they became the driving force behind other orders of chivalry in the Iberian Peninsula. The Abbey of Morimond, mother-house to Fitero in Castille, wrote the rule for the Knights of Calatrava and the Order of Alcàntara in the 1150s, while after the suppression of the Temple in 1312, Morimond took responsibility for the Order of Montesa born out of its ashes, and Alcobaça did the same in Portugal for the Order of Christ. The Cistercians also played a crucial role in the conversion to Christianity of the Baltic regions of Estonia and Latvia, thanks to the untiring efforts of Dietrich of Treiden, a monk of the Abbey of Loccum, who personally supervised the foundation of the fortified Abbey of Dünamünde in Latvia and played an important part in setting up the two military orders of the Knights of the Sword and the Knights of Dobrin in the early thirteenth century. The area also saw the creation of five nuns' convents and two more male abbeys.

The Order was in full expansion on the outer edges of Christendom just when it was slowing down to a sedate pace in the centre of the political world. In that centre the Order continued to uphold the cause of orthodoxy, standing up for the papacy against monarchs of such diverse temperament as the Emperor Frederick II in southern Italy and King John Lackland in England. By Frederick, a man of extraordinary intellect and versatility, they were to be rewarded for their honesty and constancy with the endowment of new houses.[1] King John, in his jealous anger, was to confiscate lands and wealth and generally make their life difficult until he repented and founded the magnificent abbey of Beaulieu in Hampshire.

By the thirteenth century, the Cistercian Order had become a pillar of the society it had set out to reject. King Louis IX of France filled his kingdom with abbeys for the white monks, often spending long periods of time with the community. But the abbeys he endowed were, not surprisingly, fit to entertain royalty. His favourite foundation, Royaumont near Paris, is a shining example not of simple Burgundian architecture but of the proudest, soaring Ile-de-France Gothic. The absence of a bell tower or richly-coloured glass shows nothing more than token lip-service to the

Orval, Belgium. Chapter house

OPPOSITE Le Thoronet, France. South aisle, looking east

original precepts of the Order. Soon its ambulatory was filled with royal tombs, against all the injunctions of the early Cistercian fathers. The king would, laudably, come to assist the lepers in the infirmary, pray with the monks in their stalls, beg to be allowed to wash the feet of the brothers during the Saturday *mandatum*, and generally make it impossible for the monks to avoid contact with the world.

In due course the brothers abandoned the sign language they had developed to communicate in respect for their vow of silence, and thin wooden partitions and fireplaces crept into the dormitories, making winters a little more comfortable. Meat gradually found its way into the refectory, at first under the guise of dispensations for the sick in the infirmary, but it soon became standard practice to find the thinnest of excuses in order to benefit from this sort of dispensation. In the four-teenth century, the hospitality the Order increasingly offered to travellers, together with a certain difficulty in finding sufficient vegetables, did away even with the need for an excuse and, by 1439, the General Chapter rec-ommends that meat should be eaten no more than twice a week, increas-ing to three times a week by 1486. The same Chapter of 1439 sanctioned what had obviously become standard procedure, authorizing baths for the brothers once a month and, by the seventeenth century, the monks who had prided themselves on shaving only twice a month were growing and trimming their beards into the latest fashionable shapes.

The thirteen century witnessed a radical transformation in the Order's attitudes to books and learning, thanks almost solely to the far-sighted-ness of another Stephen from England, Abbot Stephen Lexington.[2] After completing his studies at Oxford, Stephen joined the Cistercian Abbey of Quarr on the Isle of Wight and within ten years had been promoted to Abbot of Stanley in Wiltshire.

A man of considerable learning and quick intelligence, Stephen was appalled by the state of the Irish monasteries which it was his task to visit, and reached the conclusion that their unruliness could be put down to the almost total ignorance and illiteracy of their inhabitants. They spoke neither Latin nor French nor English and he was at his wits' end to find some way of communciating with them. Marked by this experience, he made it a rule that all monks, on completing their novitiate, should spend two full years studying the laws and practices of the order, with no other duties during this period to interfere with their study.

OPPOSITE Tintern, Wales. West window

Cleeve, England. Dormitory: showing spartan conditions of early Cistercian life

OPPOSITE Huerta, Spain. Refectory

Stephen went on to become Abbot of Savigny and saw his precepts applied there too. In 1227 he had already complained that a lack of great minds in the order, such as those that had filled the monasteries in the golden age of St Bernard's lifetime, was bringing it to a grave pass. 'Our order is old and vacillating,' he cried, 'soon the Dominicans will come in and take over, reforming our order with their terrible methods.' Already seven monks from Languedoc had embraced the Cathar heresy through ignorance. His pleas were apparently heard and in 1237 Everard, Abbot of Clairvaux, asked the General Chapter to authorize him to send some of his monks to the schools in Paris to study. One older monk and two lay brothers were to accompany them and take care of their material needs.

When Stephen was elected Abbot of Clairvaux in 1243, he wasted no time and, thanks to the enormous prestige that being Abbot of Clairvaux carried with it, he was able to go straight to the pope with a request to open a Cistercian college in Paris.[3] He received papal authorization almost immediately, Pope Innocent IV expressly stating that the college should be founded 'for the salvation and honour of the Cistercian order'. Stephen had aroused the jealousy of his conservative fellow abbots by going first to the pope before consulting them and then secretly asking him to send a letter to the General Chapter practically demanding that they endorse his idea. Soon after Pope Innocent IV's death, Stephen was deposed and retired to the Abbey of Ourscamp where he lived out the rest of his days in anonymity; but his college went from strength to strength despite the early hostility of the General Chapter. It was still functioning on the eve of the French Revolution and its great hall, a firemen's barracks until 1994, is one of the most beautiful buildings on the left bank of the Seine.

Two further colleges were soon founded, at the universities of Montpellier and Toulouse, and it was decreed that at least one abbey in every region should provide monks with the opportunity of studying theology. Alcobaça in Portugal built a college at the University of Coimbra, and Thame Abbey in England founded a daughter-house, the Abbey of Rewley just outside Oxford, for the sole purpose of serving as a base near the university for Cistercian students from all over the country. This was supplemented in the fifteenth century by a college of St Bernard in the town of Oxford itself. After King Henry VIII dissolved the monasteries in 1538, the college became known at St John's, and continues to function to this day under that name, with a statue of St Bernard, renamed St John, over the gateway.

Altenberg, Germany. By the fourteenth century there was little to distinguish many Cistercian abbeys from the great Gothic cathedrals

Poblet, Spain. Wash house, fountain

OPPOSITE Altenberg, Germany. North-transept window (restored)

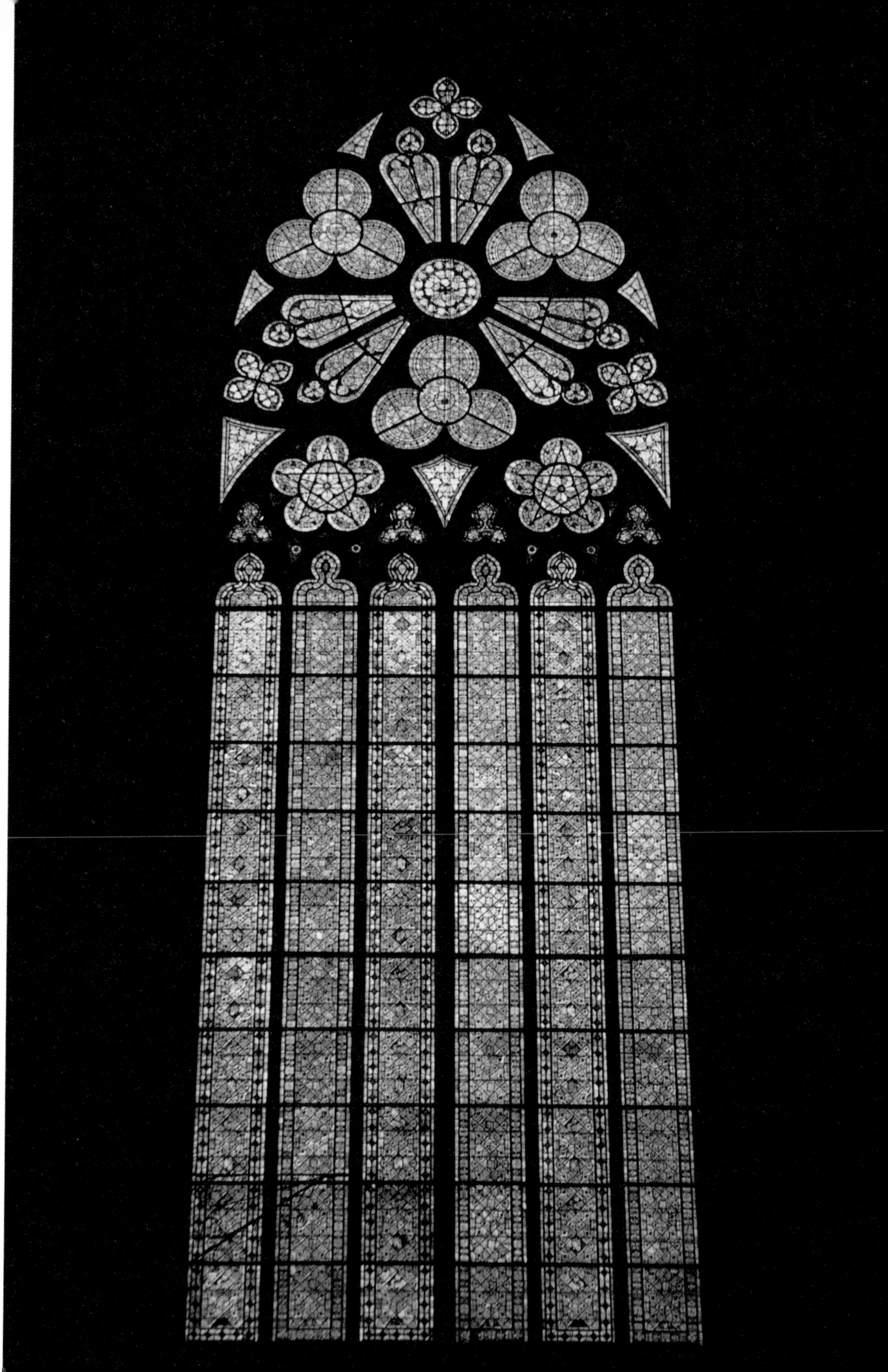

Naturally, if abbeys were to become training grounds for aspiring theologians, they needed libraries worthy of the name, and many monks' dayrooms were soon converted for this purpose. The Cistercians of the fifteenth century, in total contrast to their thirteenth century predecessors, whose suspicion of learning had brought about the downfall of Stephen Lexington, were among the first religious to adopt the newly discovered process of printing. The Abbey of Zinna in Germany and the Abbey of La Charité in France both had printing presses as early as the 1490s and, from the sixteenth century on, printing became a customary activity in many of the Order's houses.

Nor were the monks insensitive to the winds of humanism that had begun to blow over Europe from the south. Altzelle in Germany grew to become one of the centres of Renaissance learning in the March of Meissen between the fifteenth and sixteenth centuries, while in Florence the monks of the Abbey of San Salvatore a Settimo had their convent in town completely rebuilt by no less a personage than Giuliano da Sangallo, architect to Lorenzo the Magnificent; and the choir of their own abbey church is said to have been redesigned by the greatest Renaissance architect of all, Filippo Brunelleschi.

The history of the order in the century which saw the Reformation and the upheavals it produced, is one of sadness and decay. Many of the northern abbeys were destroyed and the monks murdered or martyred, during the Wars of Religion in France in the second half of the sixteenth century, and during the Dissolution of the Monasteries in England and Wales in the 1530s. It is undeniable that a certain amount of rot had set in by the early sixteenth century, providing King Henry VIII with the excuse he needed to unleash his commissioners on the 'corrupt' abbeys. In 1535, for instance, one Robert Salisbury, abbot of Valle Crucis, was known to be the ring-leader of a band of highway robbers in Oxfordshire. But sporadic gestures of heroic resistance put up by monks of the calibre of Adam Sedbergh and George Lazenby of Jervaulx or Robert Hobbes of Woburn could not halt the determination of King Henry VIII's commissioners, bent on lining their own and their sovereign's pockets with the wealth the abbeys had accumulated over 400 years.

OPPOSITE Stična, Slovenia. Refectory: restored outer wall reveals how a tall thirteenth-century refectory was first modified in the fifteenth century, then a floor was put in and the ceiling lowered in baroque times, to accommodate a library

San Galgano, Italy. View of the site from Monte Siepi. 'Bernardus valles, Benedictus montes amabat' (Bernard loved the valleys, Benedict the mountains – traditional medieval axiom). The ruined abbey of San Galgano lies deep in the valley of the river Merse, 'far from the haunts of men'

OPPOSITE Vyšší Brod, Czech Republic. The forbidding barn-like west front and tiny bellcote reflect Cistercian preoccupation with austerity (the bell tower is a later addition)

In Ireland the few foundations that had survived the wrath of Henry VIII and his daughter Elizabeth were given the final *coup de grâce* by Oliver Cromwell in the seventeenth century. In Norway and Scotland the destruction was less vicious and pursued with less vigour, but the results were the same. By the end of the 1500s not one abbey in Norway still stood, and the last surviving one in Scotland was to last only a few years into the next century. In Flanders and the Netherlands, the passage of the protestant Gueux in 1566 had spelt the end of every abbey in the area, with only feeble attempts made to restore some form of Cistercian life thereafter. The huge Abbaye des Dunes was completely razed to the ground, its bricks being used to repair the fortifications of Nieuport and Dunkirk, and it was only after many tribulations that the community managed to salvage and restore a building in the city of Bruges that had once been the property of its sister abbey Ter Doest, and start again with much reduced numbers.

In France not one of the abbeys escaped damage during the Wars of Religion. This accounts for so much conventual architecture dating from the great rebuilding of the sixteenth and seventeenth centuries. But despite the rebuilding, when the wars were over 180 abbeys had been wiped off the map for ever, and the rest were in a sorry state. Many were abandoned for ever, while others were put to the most varied uses. The fate of the Abbey of Le Reclus, in the Champagne region of France, is especially interesting. The abbey had to close due to the massacre of its monastic population and the severe damage the buildings had sustained during the Wars of Religion. But the Abbot of Clairvaux, loath to part with such a valuable property, decided to keep the premises open as a prison for recalcitrant members of the Order. From 1744 until the outbreak of the French Revolution, offending monks were sent to atone for their faults in the cells into which the former dormitory and monks' day room had been divided up. To this day visitors are still shown the elegant graffiti with which the prisoners covered the walls of their cheerless cells, whiling away the time between one service and another (for though prisoners, they were still monks and as such, bound to follow the monastic daily routine).

In Sweden, Denmark and the Protestant principalities of Germany, many of the abbey churches were converted into Protestant temples for the new religion, and owe their survival to this twist of fate. To see what

OPPOSITE Abbaye des Dunes II, Belgium. Cloister

OPPOSITE Valmagne,
France. Nave: completed in
'Ile-de-France' Gothic a
mere two years after the end
of the Albigensian crusade.
The church bears eloquent
witness to the deliberate
policy of cultural domi-
nation pursued by the
victorious French

ABOVE RIGHT
La Maigrauge, Switzerland.
Fourteenth-century choir
stalls, misericord

BELOW RIGHT
La Maigrauge, Switzerland.
Fourteenth-century choir
stalls, portraying abbey
benefactors.

a Cistercian abbey would have been like in Germany during the golden age, it is now necessary to visit the Protestant north, since in the Catholic south it is not often easy to discern the original purity of line under the heavy Baroque ornamentation with which the Cistercians 'updated' the churches they still inhabited in the eighteenth century.

To some extent the same fate befell the Italian abbeys. Cheap stucco and golden putti were applied to disguise the original lines, since most abbeys lacked the financial means to rebuild on the grand scale north of the Alps. The reason for the abbeys' disastrous financial state lies in the institution in much of Europe of a practice known as commendation. Under this system the abbacy was given by the pope or the king to a favourite or minion, or farmed out to anyone who could pay the price. The 'abbot' hardly ever resided at the abbey, was rarely a cleric, and simply used the abbey revenues for his own purposes, allowing the buildings to fall into decay. There are cases on record of the 'abbots' even selling parts of the abbey, its grounds or its buildings for their own profit. The lead from the roof of the Abbey of San Galgano in Tuscany was removed and sold by Abbot Girolamo Vitelli in the eighteenth century. Within a few years the wooden beams, stripped of their protective covering, rotted and fell through onto the vaults which promptly collapsed under the extra weight. The result is the ruin we see today.

The commendation system obviously met with much hostility, and various attempts were made to counter the decadence it invariably induced. One Martino Vargas, a monk of La Piedra in Castile, left the Order in 1427 with eleven companions, to found a new abbey at Montesion, outside Toledo. He virtually rewrote the rules governing the visitation of abbeys by the (often now commendatory) abbots of their mother-houses and greatly reinforced the authority of the prior who was elected for a three-year period and who, to all intents and purposes, took the place of the abbot. Martino's 'rebellion' incurred the displeasure of the General Chapter at Cîteaux, especially when six other Castilian abbeys embraced his reform, and he was excommunicated for insubordination. His move, however, is important in that, as well as representing an attempt to defeat the evils associated with the commendation, it was the first time in the history of the order that a grouping of abbeys assumed some sort of 'national' identity distinct from that imposed by the mother-house in France. In time Martino's family of reformed abbeys, taken back under the wing of Cîteaux at the insistence of the Pope, came to be known as the Congregation of Castile. The rising nationalism of the fifteenth century had made its mark. The European ideal, which had opposed pope and emperor for so long, had become an anachronism, and before long the entire Cistercian Order, while still owing obedience to the General Chapter at Cîteaux, was divided up into regional and national Congregations and Provinces.

No history of the Cistercians would be complete without mentioning the Congregation of Our Lady of Feuillant. A young nobleman by the name of Jean de la Barrière, whose story in some ways foreshadows that of Jean de Rancé in the following century, was made commendatory abbot of the Abbey of Feuillant, near Toulouse, in 1562 when he was only eighteen. After showing a total lack of interest in his post for some years, he converted while a student in Paris and joined the Cistercian Order, determined to wipe out the moral laxity and decadence prevalent in 'his' abbey. He did this with extraordinary success, establishing a regime which, despite its severity, attracted numerous postulants. New foundations were made and the Congregation of the Feuillants came into being. While observing the Cistercian rule in all its primitive austerity, eating only bread, water and vegetables, sleeping on boards with stones for pillows, and eating on their knees rather than off tables, the Feuillants preferred to reside in towns where they became actively involved in preaching the values of the Counter-Reformation.

But while much of Europe suffered the consequences of the Reformation, the Catholic regions of Bavaria, Swabia and Austria, Bohemia, Hungary and Poland flourished. Bell towers with brass onion bulbs rise over Burgundian naves unrecognizable in their gay baroque costume, and Gothic *Hallenkirchen* (hall churches) sport gaudy rococo disguises. Many of the abbeys were rebuilt from the foundations and are among the most dramatic examples of German baroque architecture. Schöntal, Waldsassen, Fürstenfeld, Grüssau in Poland, Rein, Schlierbach and Wilhering in Austria, are all powerful baroque churches in their own right, and there are many more abbeys where only the church remains of the medieval buildings. At Hauterive in Switzerland, a primitive Burgundian church is flanked by a majestic baroque monastery, while at Bildhausen the church was positively dwarfed by the baroque conventual buildings before it was

OVERLEAF LEFT Wilhering, Austria. Nave

OVERLEAF RIGHT Aldersbach, Germany. Nave

demolished in the last century. In the Iberian Peninsula too, many of the surviving abbeys continued to flourish. Alcobaça in Portugal and Poblet in Catalonia both reached their apogee during the eighteenth century.

This architectural renaissance was accompanied by a flowering of the liberal arts such as had never been seen before in the Cistercian Order. Music played an increasingly important part in the monastic schedule, and there are cases recorded of abbots turning their skills to the composition of polyphonic pieces for use both during divine service and for entertaining guests during dinner. To celebrate the jubilee of the Abbot of Zwettl in Austria in 1768, the services of no less a musician than Joseph Haydn were engaged to put to music a cantata written by the monks themselves. Nor was less time dedicated to the cultivation of the refined aristocratic tastes so typical of the eighteenth century in matters of art and science. The Abbey of Raitenhaslach housed a picture gallery containing 150 works by old masters, and a scientific laboratory where experiments were carried out in physics, botany, biology and zoology. Certain other abbeys even built observatories in order to encourage the study of astronomy.

And yet this dedication to worldly interests rarely detracted from the spiritual discipline and austerity of the communities. A monk from the Abbey of Heinrichau, visiting Salem Abbey in the middle of the century, was struck by the contrast between the richness of the abbey as a whole and the poverty of the individual brothers. In a monastery where one of the most well-stocked libraries in Germany boasted a librarian fluent in seven languages, where the quality of the music in the refectory at dinner excelled that offered under comparable circumstances by the cream of the local bourgeoisie, and where the sacristan had an ostensory in the treasure house worth 60,000 florins, the monks observed the strictest rules of silence, and wore the coarsest woollen underwear. He was so impressed by the austerity of the community's life style that he was prompted to say 'Here I feel I have returned to Clairvaux at the time of our father Saint Bernard'.

The revival of the order in seventeenth-century France followed an altogether different path. France was certainly not immune to the new baroque style of architecture, and at Valloires Abbey in the Pas de Calais we have the single most complete baroque Cistercian abbey still functioning as a community centre, matched only by that of Sankt Urban in Switzerland. But for the Cistercian Order, the seventeenth century in

France is of the greatest importance for reasons totally divorced from any artistic consideration. It is the century of the Abbé de Rancé and the Abbey of La Trappe.

Born in 1626, Armand Jean le Bouthillier de Rancé came from a family of the minor French nobility. Destined by birth to a life of comparative obscurity, Armand had the good fortune to have as godfather the Cardinal Richelieu. With Richelieu's rise to power, the prospects of advancement at court became distinctly brighter for the young de Rancé. Popular with the men and enjoying enviable success with the ladies of the court, thanks to his charm and wit, de Rancé soon acquired a reputation for being something of a wag and a libertine, the life and soul of court festivities.

To maintain his position he needed an appropriate income: what better than the *commende* of some prosperous or well-propertied abbey? Armand's elder brother had recently died and his benefice, the Cistercian abbey of La Trappe on the borders of Normandy, was thus vacant. It was bestowed on Richelieu's godson as a means of providing him with the sustenance he needed to maintain the estate and continue to enjoy the good living to which he had become accustomed.

But for de Rancé fate had reserved a very different road, not unlike that travelled by St Paul on the way to Damascus. The young aristocrat, saddened by the death of his love at court, retreated to his country property, where he was absolutely horrified by the state of dilapidation of the buildings and the complete moral and spiritual degeneracy of the abbey's inhabitants. Taking things firmly in hand, he started a programme of rebuilding, the results of which can still be distinguished today despite the fury vented on the abbey during the French Revolution. But, more importantly, he espoused the cause of reform which had been gaining strength in the Order since the 1570s when Jerôme de la Souchière, Abbot of Clairvaux, had taken part in the Council of Trent and decided that the Cistercians would benefit from strict application of the tenets of the Counter-Reformation, a conviction confirmed by Abbot Denis Largentier of Clairvaux in 1615.

The new reformatory movement, particularly popular among the younger members of the Order, had come to be known as the 'abstinent' movement from its most evident distinguishing feature, the return to an exclusively vegetarian diet. In reality these ardent young monks pressed for a wholesale return to the unrelenting asceticism of the first Cistercian

Fountains, England. Remains of narthex

RIGHT San Frediano al Cestello, Italy. Abbey church

fathers. With papal approval they constituted themselves into a congregation known as the 'Strict Observance', while the older monks who felt that Cistercian spirituality was not compromised by an updating of their life style came to be known as the Cistercians of the 'Common Observance'.

However, as with most schisms, the division was far from painless, and not willingly accepted by the brothers of the Common Observance, who held themselves to be the only true heirs to the teaching of St Bernard and in any case the legitimate representatives of the Cistercian Order in the world. The quarrels which ensued spanned the better part of a century, dominating the Cistercian movement throughout the 1600s. The 'Abstinents' were required to defend their cause almost continuously. In 1664 they called on a member of their congregation who, by his sudden conversion to the strictest observance of the rule after a life of dissolution and profligacy, stood as a shining example to brethren from both factions, Abbé Armand de Rancé. It may have been purely incidental that the noble background and connections of this young ex-courtier were likely to carry a lot of weight with the aristocratic College of Cardinals called to judge the issue.

In the event, de Rancé's impassioned defence of the reform movement proved indecisive, and the quarrelling dragged on for another two years before a papal bull, known as *In suprema*, officially put an end to the dispute. Brethen of both the Common and Strict Observances were to lead substantially similar lives, with the brothers of the Common Observance allowed meat three times a week except during Lent and Advent, while the reformers returned to the practice of total abstinence. Juridically the reform movement was allowed to exist as an independent structure, with its own abbots as visitors and a share in the university colleges, as well as the right to assign ten abbots to the executive committee of the General Chapter. But it still remained under the wing, and watchful eye, of the Annual General Chapter at Cîteaux. For de Rancé, this made a mockery of everything he had fought for. His violent temper and blinkered sense of morality got the better of him and he denounced the papal bull as an attempt to clip the movement's wings and reduce it to impotence. One cannot but speculate that, had he fought less and tried more gentle persuasion, the Order might have been reformed and reconciled at the same time rather than split into two groupings which still look askance at each other today.

Be that as it may, de Rancé imposed an extremely strict lifestyle on his own monks at La Trappe, stricter even than that of the original fathers at Cîteaux. He not only forbade the eating of meat, but also of fish, eggs, cheese and butter. His attitude towards life in the monastery betrayed an obsession with sin and repentance which can be traced back to his profligate youth.

No one really doubts the good faith and piety of de Rancé but his excessive religious zeal has the taint of fanaticism. Often called by his own disciples the 'second St Bernard', he appears rather to represent the panicky post-Tridentine asceticism of his century which expressed itself more through the Inquisition and witch-hunts than through any mystical aspiration to unity with God. And yet his work survived, and the family of the Strict Observance prospered. By the time of the French Revolution there were sixty-five abbeys, by now with their own General Chapter and a much greater degree of independence from Cîteaux, answering to the name of Trappist.

The eighteenth century spelled the end of the great adventure. In 1782 the Habsburg Emperor Joseph II ordered all 'useless religious institutions' closed. In the age of illuminism, this enlightened monarch considered contemplative monasticism a waste of time. Luckily for posterity this move was made by an intelligent and ageing man. No Tudor greed bent on gain nor popular fury venting its spleen was to wreak the destruction visited on the monasteries during the English dissolution or the French Wars of Religion. The houses were closed and their occupants pensioned off. The buildings were simply put to secular use and many of the churches became parish churches serving local communities.

In the outer reaches of the Empire, in Belgium for instance, such abbeys as had survived the sixteenth-century wars managed to outlive the Emperor Joseph as well. He died before his decree could be fully implemented. But what had at first appeared to be a stroke of luck proved in the event to be fatal. Only seven years after the Habsburg decree, the outbreak of revolution in France sealed the fate of the Cistercian Order.

Regarded by the populace and the bourgeoisie as bulwarks of privilege and bastions of reaction, the monasteries and religious institutions were among the first targets of the revolutionary fury. While there was undoubtedly some truth in this belief, it is hard to excuse the wholesale destruction of over ninety per cent of some of the finest medieval architecture ever created. The late eighteenth and early nineteenth centuries

saw speculation and greed rest their eye on these superb quarries of ready-cut stone, and demolish them in the name of equality, liberty and fraternity, from Languedoc to Belgium, from Brittany to the Franche-Comté and, during the Napoleonic invasions, down into Italy and Spain too.

While speculation on the part of local businessmen accounted for most of the destruction, in some cases we hear of the pointless torture of the two or three venerable old men still clinging pathetically to their vocations, the only inhabitants of their decaying monasteries. At the Abbey of Mortemer in Normandy, visitors are still shown the cellar in which the last two brothers, aged well into their eighties, were tortured and finally starved to death. At Royaumont near Paris, the former keeper of Queen Marie Antoinette's gaming purse, who had bought the abbey at auction, demonstrated his republican fervour by wantonly tearing down, stone by stone, the vast Gothic church 'built by one of our late tyrants', and then boasting about it to the National Assembly who suspected him, probably rightly, of royalist sympathies.

The greater part of the abbeys sold at auction appealed to the bourgeoisie and what was left of the minor aristocracy because it offered them a chance to recoup most of their initial capital outlay by selling off cut stone from the church they demolished, and turning the often recently rebuilt Renaissance and baroque conventual buildings into stylish manors and châteaux at little cost and with great speed. Many an abbot's lodging provided the perfect 'gentilhommière', and the famed Cistercian fruit orchards, woods, arable land and, most of all, their vineyards, proved very attractive to the rising class of newly rich entrepreneurs who were to characterize the nineteenth century.

The procedure of suppression and the sale of abbey possessions is particularly well documented in the case of the mother-house itself, Cîteaux. In May 1790, inventories were taken of all the abbey property and the monks assembled and asked whether they were content with the pension being offered them. Fourteen monks, including Abbot François Trouvé, replied indignantly that they wanted to continue in the religious life, while twenty-nine others stated that they would happily accept the pension and return to their civilian status; two were unsure. Between September of 1790 and January of the following year, most of the monks

OPPOSITE Royaumont, France. Cloister, north walk

OVERLEAF Elan, France. Abbot's lodgings, fifteenth century

departed the abbey with their pensions and the rest were thrown out since, by then, the property had been sold, the sale going through on 24 March for the sum of £482,000. The local populace took the fall of the abbey as a signal to join in the free-for-all and grab as much as they could with impunity. Things not unnaturally took a violent turn and an artillery squad, under the command of one Napoleon Bonaparte, was called in to quell the riots.

Abbot Trouvé retired to the house of his nephew in Vosne, from where he wrote to the seat of the Order in Rome, the Abbey of Santa Croce in Gerusalemme, delegating all his powers to the Procurator General of the order with the Holy See, Abbot Alano Bagatti. In 1797 he died in the little house in Vosne, after writing the last chapter of a story that had begun 700 years earlier, almost to the day, when Robert of Molesme had set out from his abbey to try and find God in a desolate wilderness near Vosne, called Cîteaux.

OPPOSITE Royaumont, France. All that remains of the abbey church after the Revolution

After the Storm: 1789 to the Present Day

T HE STORY OF THE CISTERCIAN ORDER following the cata-
clysm of the French Revolution is a story of determination and
single-mindedness bordering often on the heroic; in fact it is
probably the closest thing to a return to the original intentions
of the founding fathers since de Rancé had rebelled against the laxity of
the order in the seventeenth century. Thus it is no mere chance that we
find the Trappists, who prior to the Revolution had been a minority in
the order, leading the movement to revive the Cistercian ideal.

The reign of terror in which the French Revolution had culminated,
had created a widespread feeling of disillusionment with the 'enlightened'
ideals which had fostered it. Society as a whole became more sympathetic
to both the spiritual ideals which had inspired the Cistercian way of life
and to the material remains of that lifestyle. Our appreciation of ivy-clad
ruins can of course be traced back, in part, to the eighteenth century and
the birth of the Romantic movement, but it is perhaps less widely acknowledged that the cultural climate which favoured the development of
the Romantic ideal was also responsible for allowing the resurrection of
monastic life.

The last novice master before the Revolution at the Abbey of La Trappe
had been a certain Dom Augustin Lestrange. When the abbey was requi-
sitioned and the monks expelled, Lestrange, acting under the authority of
Abbot Trouvé of Cîteaux and Abbot Rocourt of Clairvaux, had fled to
Switzerland taking twenty-one monks with him. The government of the
Canton of Fribourg allowed him to settle with his small community in
the abandoned charterhouse of La Valsainte near Gruyères, and it was
here, in 1791, that the flame of Cistercian life was rekindled. At the time,
Lestrange and his group of faithful followers simply sought to prevent

that flame from being extinguished altogether, implementing in their almost frantic attempts to preserve their way of life a series of rules which were, if anything, even more stringent than those laid down by de Rancé. In their Alpine stronghold the monks dispensed with all forms of heating, slept on rough planks with a single coverlet, ate nothing but bread and boiled pulses, drank only water and spent at least twelve hours a day in church. The rest of the day was equally divided between sleep and manual labour. Contrary to Lestrange's expectations, the severity of this life style attracted a fair number of vocations and, in 1794, the community was authorized by the pope to elect an abbot, the choice falling naturally on Lestrange.

The elders of the Canton of Fribourg had specified that the community of La Valsainte should not exceed twenty-four in number. Thus, in best Cistercian tradition, Lestrange began sending monks off to wherever he thought, or had been informed, that the climate was right for founding daughter-houses. While the preparation of these monks was at best somewhat cursory, a fact readily excused by the critical nature of the times, they were by no means lacking in ardour and determination. Twice, pioneering groups of three or four brothers set out for Canada, but on both occasions failed to reach their destination. The political upheavals dominating European affairs in the late eighteenth century prevented the first group from leaving continental Europe: they got no further than Amsterdam, where they founded a monastery in a farmhouse near Westmalle, only to be moved on a few years later by the invading armies of France, ending up in Darfeld in Westphalia.

The second group reached England but made no further progress. They set up house in Lulworth on the Dorset coast, where their abbey, the first founded in England since the sixteenth-century Reformation, survived until 1817. After the defeat of Napoleon and the lifting of the ban on religious communities in France, the monks returned to their native land and restored the old Cistercian abbey of Melleray in Brittany, where the Trappist community is still very much a part of the local scene. Melleray itself was able, after only twenty years, to found two new daughter-houses in the British Isles, Mount St Bernard in Leicestershire and Mount Melleray in Ireland; these too are still active centres of monastic life today.

Meanwhile, the attitude which had caused the Habsburg Emperor Joseph II in 1782 to insist that all monasteries demonstrate their social usefulness was still a decisive component of the contemporary cultural climate, and Lestrange felt it incumbent upon him to subscribe at least in part to that philosophy. He opened a school for local boys at La Valsainte and founded the Trappist third order for sympathetic laymen who wished to live in spiritual communion with the precepts of the order but were unable, for one reason or another, to take full monastic vows; at the same time, he encouraged refugee nuns in other parts of Switzerland to found similar schools for girls. But when Switzerland was invaded by the French Revolutionary armies in 1798, Lestrange was forced once again to take to the road, this time with a monastic family of over 250 people including monks, nuns, members of the third order (or tertiaries as they were called) and children from the monastic schools.

At the invitation of the Czar of Russia, this ragged band of refugees started out on an odyssey that was to last almost two years, earning the admiration even of Napoleon Bonaparte. Reaching Belarus after six months, the restless Lestrange failed to find the welcome he had expected and turned his thoughts once more to the New World. The group took ship at Danzig but was forced ashore by a storm at Lübeck, where many of the monks, disheartened by the succession of misfortunes, left to join their former comrades in Darfeld. Others returned to La Valsainte, following the reconciliation between Pope Pius VII and Napoleon, while only a small number continued with the plan to cross the Atlantic, founding the first Cistercian community on American soil in Baltimore in 1803.

Renewed hostilities between France and the papacy in 1809 caused the French authorities to clamp down once more on religious houses and Lestrange was arrested, but he managed to escape and make his way to New York, where he purchased some land with the intention of founding, at last, the community of which he had dreamed since first fleeing La Trappe some twenty years before. The fall of Napoleon only three years later, however, enabled him to return to Europe and so nothing came of his plans, but the land he had bought on the island of Manhattan remained church property: on it now stands St Patrick's, the cathedral church of New York City.

The expansion of the Trappists after the downfall of Napoleon and the virtual re-establishment of religious freedom in much of Europe was extraordinary. Lestrange was able to restore his own Abbey of La Trappe

OPPOSITE ABOVE Cîteaux, France. The disappointing modern church now occupying the site of Cîteaux

OPPOSITE BELOW La Valsainte, Switzerland. Nave

and further foundations soon followed, including the Port-du-Salut, where the monks ensured their economic survival by selling the cheese they made from the rich milk provided by their herd of cattle. Within Lestrange's lifetime the abbeys of Melleray, Aiguebelle, Bellefontaine, Bellevaux and Notre-Dame-du Gard had been added in France, and the community of Darfeld had founded Olenberg in Alsace. By 1825 there were eleven male and five female monasteries in Europe, as well as two schools run by the tertiaries. Thirty years later the male monasteries had reached a total of twenty-three, including two in America and one in Algeria, and by the end of the century the order counted more than twice that number. In 1894, 3,000 Trappist monks were living a regular monastic life in accordance with the precepts of the founding fathers of the Cistercian Order as interpreted by the Abbé de Rancé. The abbeys they founded reached from their native France, through Germany and the Austro-Hungarian Empire, Italy, Spain and England, Holland and Ireland, to Canada, Australia, South Africa and China.

Lestrange's last years were embittered by the realization that the rule he had enjoined upon his followers in the heroic days of La Valsainte was too harsh for any realistic expectation that it would be adhered to in all its severity by the growing Trappist family. As early as 1815 the Abbot of Darfeld, Dom Eugène de Laprade, had successfully petitioned the pope for his community to be allowed to return to the milder prescriptions of de Rancé. There ensued more than half a century of what can only be described as petty bickering, with abbeys adhering to one or the other 'observance' according to which way the wind blew in Rome, and delegations nominated by one or the other tendency trying to win papal approval. By the late 1860s the Trappist movement had officially split into two separate congregations, known as the 'Old Reform', comprising those abbeys that had returned to the interpretation of de Rancé, and the 'New Reform', which grouped together the adherents of Lestrange. It was not until 1892 that the two tendencies were once again reunited under the denomination of 'Order of the Reformed Cistercians and of Our Lady of La Trappe', thanks largely to the efforts of Abbot Sebastian Wyart of the Abbey of Sept-Fons in Burgundy.

Abbot Wyart's success was to be crowned by the Trappist's purchase in 1898 of the first mother-house of the order, Cîteaux itself. The monastery and church had been completely destroyed during the Revolution, but the new community restored the eighteenth-century wing, which had been spared any major damage, and built a new church on the site of Stephen Harding's original cluster of buildings. The white monks had come home and, in recognition of this, the name of La Trappe was dropped from their title. While they are still unofficially known as Trappists even today, the order, which counts eighty abbeys and some 3,400 monks, was solemnly renamed by papal decree in 1902 the 'Order of the Reformed Cistercians of the Strict Observance', and recognized to be the true heir to the spiritual values of the pioneer monks who had first settled at Cîteaux.

Heir to the legal and material as well as the spiritual inheritance of Cîteaux, on the other hand, was the 'Common Observance'. Recognized as such by the Holy See immediately after the Revolution, the order was only very loosely organized in a series of national congregations which had managed to survive the storm. Communications between these independent congregations were so difficult as to be almost non-existent. Not only did the very supranational nature of organizations such as the Cistercian Order arouse suspicion in the heavily nationalistic climate prevalent throughout the nineteenth century, but most of the conservative-oriented governments which took office in Europe after the downfall of Napoleon, though not specifically anti-clerical, were hostile to what Emperor Joseph II had termed socially 'useless' monastic orders.

The papacy obviously encouraged the rebirth of the Cistercians: at Santa Croce in Gerusalemme, Rome, and at Casamari; while the pro-Catholic government of the new state of Belgium favoured the purchase of the ruins of Val-Dieu, near Liège, by the abbey's last surviving monk, Bernhard Klinkenberg. All three abbeys are still active centres of monastic life today. Abbé Léon Barnouin bought the disused buildings of Sénanque in Provence and, in 1855, in honour of the recently instituted dogma of the Immaculate Conception, he founded the Congregation which took its name from the abbey. Within a few years the Congregation of Sénanque had restored three more abbeys on French soil.

The thirteen or so abbeys that had survived Emperor Joseph II's blitz against the contemplative orders were reduced, despite their buoyancy in terms of vocations, to little more than appendages of the secular clergy. Still required to demonstrate their social usefulness, they devoted their energies almost exclusively to teaching and pastoral work. Typically, the Hungarian Abbey of Zirc had to care for twelve parishes as well as running three schools, and all with a complement of thirty-five monks. Understandably, the monks had little time left to perform the liturgical obligations enjoined upon them or to live anything approaching the sort of monastic life envisioned by the founding fathers. The government adopted a form of 'pincer' strategy to strengthen its grip on the abbeys: all novices were obliged to attend state-approved seminars where government policy was forcefully propounded, while no abbey was allowed to entertain relations with other Cistercian abbeys in the Empire or with the mother-house in Rome. The revolution of 1848 softened the government's attitude towards the Church, and the Austro-Hungarian 'congregation' was able to make contact with the Order's abbot president, and efforts to restore a degree of traditional monastic discipline resulted in the publication of the Statutes of Prague ten years later. While these statutes were never officially ratified, they mark a turning point in the history of the Common Observance. They represent the first real steps within the Order towards reconciling traditional contemplative monasticism with what we today might term 'social commitment'.

Despite numerous encounters, negotiations and appeals to outside jurisdiction throughout the rest of the century, however, no real progress was made towards a reunification of the Common Observance, although the individual congregations were in a position, from the point of view of vocations, that it would be difficult to call unhealthy. Their numbers were on the increase in all three provinces: Austria-Hungary, France and Belgium, but that their principal concern was of a pastoral and intellectual nature can be deduced from the almost total absence of lay brothers, that ancient institution which had characterized the Order for so long, and the high proportion of priests. While the Trappists counted more than 2,000 lay brothers at the end of the century, the Common Observance had a total of 146. On the other hand, the abbeys of the Common Observance catered for more than 250,000 souls in the parishes under their care, as well as running numerous schools at all levels, many of which were reputed to provide the best education available.

Today the Cistercian Order of the Common Observance, grouped in tightly knit regional or national congregations and united once again, since 1933, under the central authority of an Abbot General, is a thriving religious institution. Present in force in North and South America, Australia and the Far East as well as in Italy, France, Spain, Switzerland, Germany, Austria and Slovenia, the Order is currently engaged in restoring some of its abbeys in the former Iron Curtain countries, determined to keep alive the flame lit by Robert of Molesme 900 years ago.

A Description of Clairvaux

SHOULD YOU WISH to picture Clairvaux, the following has been written to serve you as a mirror. Imagine two hills and between them a narrow valley, which widens out as it approaches the monastery. The abbey covers the half of one hillside and the whole of the other. With one rich in vineyards, the other in crops, they do double duty, gladdening the heart and serving our necessities, one shelving flank providing food, the other drink. On the ridges themselves it is often the monks' work (pleasant indeed and the more so for being peaceful) to collect dead brushwood and tie it in bundles for burning, sorting out the prickly brambles and cutting and tying only what is fit for the fires. Their job too to grub out the briars, to uproot and destroy what Solomon calls the bastard slips, which throttle the growing branches or loosen the roots, lest the stout oak be hindered from saluting the height of heaven, the lime from deploying its supple branches, the pliant ash that splits so readily from growing freely upwards, the fan-shaped beech from attaining its full spread.

Farther on, the rear of the abbey extends to the wide valley bottom, much of which lies inside the great sweep of the abbey wall. Within this cincture many fruit-bearing trees of various species make a veritable grove of orchards, which by their nearness to the infirmary afford no small solace to the brothers in their sickness: a spacious promenade for those able to walk, an easeful resting-place for the feverish. The sick man sits on the green turf, and, when the merciless heat of the dog days bakes the fields and dries up the streams, he in his sanctuary, shaded from the day's heat, filters the heavenly fire through a screen of leaves, his discomfort further eased by the drifting scent of the grasses. While he feeds his gaze on the pleasing green of grass and trees, fruits, to further his delight, hang swelling before his eyes, so that he can not inaptly say: 'I sat in the shadow of his tree, which I had desired, and its fruit was sweet to my taste.' A chorus of brightly feathered birds caresses his ears with sweetest melody. Thus for a single illness God in his goodness provides many a soothing balm: the sky smiles serene and clear, the earth quivers with life, and the sick man drinks in, with eyes, ears and nostrils, the delights of colour, song and scent.

Where the orchard ends the garden begins, marked out into rectangles, or, more accurately, divided up by a network of streamlets; for, although the water appears asleep, it is in fact slipping slowly away. Here too a pretty spectacle is afforded to the sick, who can sit on the grassy banks of the clear runnels watching the fish at play in the translucent water, their manoeuvres recalling troops in battle. This water, which serves the dual purpose of feeding the fish and irrigating the vegetables, is supplied by the tireless course of the river Aube, of famous name, which flows through the many workshops of the abbey. Wherever it passes it evokes a blessing in its wake, proportionate to its good offices; for it does not slip through unscathed or at its leisure, but at the cost of much exertion. By means of a winding channel cut through the middle of the valley, not by nature but by the hard work of the brethren, the Aube sends half its waters into the monastery, as though to greet the monks and apologize for not having come in its entirety, for want of a bed wide enough to carry its full flow. And should this stream in spate surge forward in a tumultuous sally, re-pulsed by the fronting wall under which it has to flow, it falls back into itself, and the current once again embraces the reflux. As much of the stream as this wall, acting as gatekeeper, allows in by the sluice-gates hurls itself initially with swirling force against the mill, where its ever-increasing turbulence, harnessed first to the weight of the millstones and next to the fine-meshed sieve, grinds the grain and then separates the flour from the bran.

The stream now fills the cauldron in a nearby building and suffers itself to be boiled to prepare the brothers' drink (should husbandry have been ill-rewarded by a poor vintage, and malt, in default of grape juice, have to supply the want). Nor does it hold itself acquitted yet. The fullers, next door to the mill, invite it in, claiming with reason on their side that, if it swirls and eddies in the mill, which provides the brothers with food, it should do no less by those who clothe them. The stream does not demur, nor indeed refuse any request made of it. Instead, raising and lowering by turns the heavy pestles (unless you prefer the term mallets or, better still, wooden feet – the expression which seems most suited to the gymnastic occupation of the fullers), it frees these brothers from their drudgery. And should their gravity be broken by some jest, it frees them too from punishment for their sin. O Lord, how great are the consolations that you in your goodness provide for your poor servants, lest a greater wretchedness engulf them! How generously you palliate the hardships of your penitents, lest perchance they be crushed at times by the harshness of their toil! From how much back-breaking travail for horses and arm-aching labour for men does this obliging torrent free us, to the extent that without it we should be neither clothed nor fed. It is most truly shared with us, and expects no other reward wheresoever it toils under the sun than that, its work done, it be allowed to run freely away. So it is that, after driving so many noisy and swiftly spinning wheels, it flows out foaming, as though it too had been ground and softened in the process.

The tannery is next to capture the stream, and here it displays its zeal in the fashioning of all that goes to make the brothers' footwear. Thereafter, its water decanted into a succession of channels, it carries out a dutiful inspection of each workshop, diligently inquiring where it can be of service and offering its ungrudging help in the work of cooking, sifting, turning, whetting, watering, washing, grinding and softening. Lastly, to ensure that no cause for gratitude be wanting, that its tasks be left in no respect unfinished, it carries the waste products away and leaves everything clean in its wake, and, while Clairvaux renders it thanks for all its blessings, it courteously returns the abbey's greetings as it hastens away to pour back into the river the waters siphoned off into the monastery. The two currents are indistinguishably mingled and the river, shrunken and sluggish since the diversion, surges forward under the onrush of water.

Now that we have returned the stream to its bed, let us go back to those rills we left behind. They too are diverted from the river and meander placidly through the meadows, saturating the soil that it may germinate. And when, with the coming of the mild spring weather, the pregnant earth gives birth, they keep it watered too lest the springing grasses should wither for lack of moisture. As it is, these have no need to depend on drops begged from the clouds, fostered as they are by the care of the kindred river. These rills, or more properly trenches, their job done, are swallowed once more by the river that spewed them forth, and the Aube, now fully replenished, rushes off on its steep downhill course. And we, who have kept it company all this way, until it, in Solomon's words, has returned to its place, let us too return to our point of departure and, wasting no words, leap lightly over the wide expanse of the meadow.

Here is a spot that has much to delight the eye, to revive the weak spirit, to soothe the aching heart and to arouse to devotion all who seek the Lord. It brings to mind the heavenly bliss to which we all aspire, for the smiling face of the earth with its many hues feasts the eyes and breathes sweet scents into the nostrils. Both the sight and the scent of the meadow put me in mind of tales of long ago. Their scent recalls to me that the smell of Jacob's garments was compared to the fragrance of a fertile field; their colour, how the splendour of Solomon's purple was displayed. And yet he, who lacked neither the skill derived from wisdom nor the means that power affords, could not in all his glory rival the lilies of the field. And so it is that, while agreeably employed in the open, I get no little pleasure from the mystery beneath the surface.

This meadow is refreshed by the floodwaters of the Aube, which runs through it, so that the grass, thanks to the moisture at its roots, can stand the summer heat. Its extent is great enough to tire the community for the space of twenty days when the sun has baked to hay its shorn grassy fleece. Nor is the haymaking left to the monks alone: alongside them a countless multitude of lay-brothers and voluntary and hired helpers gather the mown grass and comb the shorn ground with wide-toothed rakes.

Two granges divide this meadow between them, the Aube serving as an equitable judge and surveyor in the settling of disputes. Assigning to each its share, like a marking-rope it sets the bounds that neither dares cross to invade the other's portion. You would take these granges not for the living quarters of lay-brothers but for monastic cloisters were it not that ox-yokes, ploughs and other farm implements betray the inhabitants' status, and that no books are opened there. As regards the monastic buildings themselves, you will admit that they are well-fitted in size, siting and appearance to a large community of monks.

In the part of the meadow nearest the wall, a watery lake has been created from the solid field. Where in former times the sweating labourer mowed the hay with a sharp scythe, today the brother in charge of the fish-ponds, seated on a wooden horse, is borne over the smooth surface of this liquid field. Wherever he goes, a light pole serves him for spurs to speed his progress, for a curb when turning. The net destined to entangle the fish is spread under the water, and its favourite baits are set, but primed with a hidden hook to catch the unwary — an example which teaches us to spurn delights, for pleasure harms and suffering is its price. Only the man who has never sinned or never done true penance for sin can possibly ignore that the outcome of pleasure is pain. May God keep pleasure far removed from us – that pleasure at whose doorway death stands posted, and which a wise man likens to bees on the wing, which, as soon as they have shed their sweet burden of honey, turn and strike the addicted heart with a deep-seated sting. The high bank surrounding the mere is faced with wattle made from withy roots to prevent the soil from slipping into the water that washes it. A brook some thirty feet distant keeps the water-level constant by means of feeder ditches, which carry and regulate both inflow and outflow.

But while I am winging my way across the plain, breathless with the exertion, whether it be describing the vivid surface of the meadow painted by Wisdom's own hand or the ridges of the hills with their shaggy pelt of trees, I am taxed with ingratitude by that sweet spring from which I have drunk times without number and whose deserts I have ill requited. It has often quenched my thirst, humbled itself to wash not only my hands but my feet, and done me many a kindness and service – good offices which merited a better reward. For now it reproaches me bitterly with having assigned it the last place, and that only just, in my topographical list, when the first, by right of reverence, was its due. And indeed I cannot deny that my memory was laggard when it gave others precedence. This spring, like the waters of Siloam which move silently, glides to and fro unheard down subterranean channels. Its course cannot be detected by the faintest murmur, and, as though it feared discovery, it hangs its head and turns its face aside. Why should I not think it wanted to be passed over in silence when it secretes itself under cover? Like all good springs it sallies out over against the rising sun, so that midsummer finds it greeting the roseate splendour of dawn full in the face. A small but pretty hut, or tabernacle to use a more reverential word, encloses it and protects it from any dirt. It wells out of the hillside only to be swallowed by the valley, and in the very place of its birth it seems to die, nay, even to be buried. But do not look for the sign of Jonah the prophet, expecting it to lie hidden away for three days and three nights: at once a thousand feet away, it rises again in the abbey cloister, as it might be from the bowels of the earth, and, as it were restored to life, offers itself to the sight and use of the brethren, lest its future lot should be with any but the holy.

Written by an anonymous twelfth-century monk

Translated and edited by Pauline Matarasso for 'The Cistercian World: Monastic Writing of the Twelfth Century', pp 287–92. Penguin Classics, 1993. Copyright © Pauline Matarasso, 1993.

Appendix B
The Abbeys: A Gazetteer

A complete list of male Cistercian abbeys founded between 1118 and 1390. Where the remains warrant, nunneries (indicated by Roman numerals) and granges (indicated by a letter) are included.

Key

Abbey Name by which the abbey is most commonly known today (alternative names are in brackets).

*NB: An * after the name indicates that the abbey, whatever its condition, is especially rewarding to visit.*

Condition   0 = Site unknown
1 = Site known, but little or nothing remains
2 = Some ruins visible

or

The buildings on the site are unrelated to the original abbey structure
3 = Considerable remains
4 = Reasonably complete

or

What few buildings remain are intact
5 = The abbey is virtually complete
(but no longer a place of worship)
6 = Still a place of worship
(the abbey is not necessarily intact)

Style   – = The remains, if any, are so insubstantial, as not to warrant definition
c = Early Cistercian (sometimes defined as 'Transitional Romanesque/Gothic')
R = Romanesque

G = Gothic
I = Renaissance
B = Baroque or Rococo
M = Modern (including neo-Romanesque, neo-Gothic etc.)

NB: A combination of two or more letters (eg. C-G-B) indicates that more than one style will be found at the site

Accessibility   0 = Not accessible to the public
1 = Outside only visible to the public
2 = Not normally open to the public (a prior phone call or polite request *may* get you in!)
3 = Some parts open to the public at given times
4 = Accessible to the public during opening hours (which may be seasonal)
5 = As above, with leaflet available at site, guided tours etc. (and possibly an entry fee)

I. For the convenience of the modern traveller, this gazetteer is broken down by country within current boundaries.

II. Every attempt has been made to keep the gazetteer as accurate as possible. Constantly changing conditions, however, whether political, cultural or religious, make this an extraordinarily difficult task. Readers' comments and indications will be most welcome, and will be taken into account in future editions of this book.

III. Where I have been unable to find any information concerning the current state of a particular abbey, I have been forced to leave the entry blank. Any information concerning those abbeys from readers who have personal knowledge of them, will be most welcome and will be incorporated (with appropriate acknowledgement of the source) in future editions of this book.

Abbey	Map Ref.	Con-dition	Style	Accessi-bility
AUSTRIA (map p. 223)				
BAUMGARTENBERG	1	6	C-G-B	3
ENGELZELL	2	6	G-B	3
HEILIGENKREUZ*	3	6	R-G	5
LILIENFELD*	4	6	C-B	3
MARIENFELD (Bors Monostra)	5	6	C-B	4
NEUBERG*	6	6	G	4
NEUKLOSTER	7	6	G-B	3
REIN	8	6	B	3
SÄUSENSTEIN	9	2	G-B	4
SCHLÄGL	10	6	C-G-B	5
SCHLIERBACH	11	6	B	5
STAMS	12	6	B	5
VIKTRING	13	6	C-G-B	4
WILHERING	14	6	C-B	5
ZWETTL*	15	6	C-G	5
BELGIUM (map p. 227)				
AULNE*	16	3	C-G-B	3
BAUDELOO	17	1	G	4
CAMBRON-CASTEAU	18	2	C-B	5
Ter DOEST (barn only)*	19	5	C	4
Ter DUINEN (Abbaye des Dunes)	20	3	G	5
Ter DUINEN (II)	20a	6	B	3
GRANDPRE	21	4	B	2
HOCHT	22	3	G-B	2
MOULINS	23	4	C-B-M	2
ORVAL*	24	6	C-M	5
St. BERNAERDS-op't-SCHELT	25	4	B	3
VAL-DIEU	26	6	G-M	3
VAL St LAMBERT	27	4	C-B	3
VILLERS-la-VILLE	28	4	C-G-B	5
De BIJLOKE	I	5	G-B	5
La CAMBRE (Ter Kameren)	II	5	G-B	3

Abbey	Map Ref.	Con- dition	Style	Accessi- bility
CROATIA (map p. 222)				
TOPLICA	745	2	C	4
VALLIS HONESTA (Kutjevo, Pozega)	746	I	—	4
ZAGRABIA (Insula Save)	747	6	B	4
CYPRUS (map p. 230)				
BEAULIEU	43	I	C-G	4
CZECH REPUBLIC (map p. 223)				
MNICHOVO HRADISTE (Münchengrätz)	29	2	C	3
NEPOMUK	30	2	C	4
OSEK (Ossegg)*	31	6	C-G-B	5
PLASY (Plass)	32	6	G-B	2
SEDLEC (Sedletz)*	33	6	G-B	4
SKALICE KLASTERSKA (Skalitz)	34	2	G-B	2
SVATE POLE (Heiligenfeld)	35	I	—	4
VELEHRAD	37	6	R-B	3
VYSSI BROD (Hohenfurt)*	38	6	C-G	5
VIZOVICE (Wisowitz)	39	I	—	2
ZBRASLAV (Königsaal)	40	5	G-B	3
ZDAR (Saar)	41	6	G-B	3
ZLATA KORUNA (Goldenkron)*	42	6	C-G	5
OSLAVANY	III	6	C-B	3
TISNOV	IV	6	R-C	4
DENMARK (map p. 228)				
ESROM	44	2	C	I
HOLME*	45	6	C-B	3
KNARDRUP	46	I	—	4
LØGUMKLOSTER*	47	6	C	5
ØMKLOSTER	48	2	C	5
SORØ*	49	6	C-B	3
TVIS	50	I	—	4
VITSKØL	51	4	C-B	5

Abbey	Map Ref.	Con- dition	Style	Accessi- bility
ENGLAND (map p. 220)				
BEAULIEU	52	3	C-G	5
BIDDLESDEN	53	1	—	1
BINDON (Woolbridge)	54	2	C-G	1
BORDESLEY	55	2	C	5
BOXLEY	56	2	C	0
BRUERN	57	1	—	0
BUCKFAST	58	2	G	3
BUCKLAND	59	3	C-G	5
BUILDWAS*	60	4	C	5
BYLAND*	61	3	C-G	5
CALDER	62	3	C	1
CLEEVE*	63	4	G	5
COGGESHALL	64	2	C-G	0
COMBE	65	3	R-C	5
COMBERMERE	66	1	—	0
CROXDEN	67	3	C	5
DIEULACRES	68	2	G	0
Abbey DORE*	69	6	C	5
DUNKESWELL	70	1	—	4
FLAXLEY	71	2	C-G	2
FORDE*	72	4	C-G	5
FOUNTAINS*	73	4	C-G	5
FURNESS*	74	4	R-C-G	5
GARENDON	75	1	C	0
GRACE DIEU	76	1	—	4
HAILES	77	3	G	5
HOLMCULTRAM	78	6	R-C	5
Abbey HULTON	79	1	G	4
JERVAULX	80	3	C-G	5
KINGSWOOD (*gatehouse only*)	81	4	G-I	4
KIRKSTALL*	82	4	R-C-G	3
KIRKSTEAD (*gate chapel only*)	83	6	C	4
LOUTH PARK	84	1	—	1
LULWORTH (Little Bindon)	85	1	R	1
MEAUX	86	1	—	4
MEDMENHAM	87	2	G	0
MEREVALE	88	2	C	0

Abbey	Map Ref.	Con-dition	Style	Accessi-bility
NETLEY*	89	4	C-G	5
NEWENHAM	90	1	—	1
NEWMINSTER	91	2	C	4
PIPEWELL	92	1	—	2
QUARR	93	2	C	5
REVESBY	94	1	—	4
REWLEY	95	1	G	4
RIEVAULX*	96	4	C-G	5
ROBERTSBRIDGE	97	2	C	1
ROCHE*	98	3	C	5
RUFFORD	99	3	C	5
ST MARY GRACES (Eastminster)	100	1	G	2
SALLEY	101	3	C	5
SAWTREY	102	1	—	4
SIBTON	103	2	C-G	2
STANLEY	104	1	—	4
STOCKING	105	1	R	1
STONELEIGH	106	3	G	2
STRATFORD LANGTHORNE	107	1	G	0
SWINESHEAD	108	1	—	1
THAME	109	2	G	0
TILTY (gate chapel only)	110	4	C-G	4
VALE ROYAL	111	1	M-C	3
VAUDEY	112	1	—	0
WARDEN	113	1	G-I	1
WAVERLEY	114	2	C-G	4
WHALLEY*	115	4	C-G	5
WOBURN	116	1	—	5
GREAT COXWELL	A	5	C	5

ESTONIA (map p. 228)

FALKENAU	726	2	C	1
PADIS	727	6	G	1

FRANCE (map p. 221)

ACEY	117	6	C-B	2
AIGUEBELLE*	118	6	C	2

Abbey	Map Ref.	Con-dition	Style	Accessi-bility
ARDOREL	119	2	C	0
AUBEPIERRES	120	2	—	2
AUBERIVE	121	5	C-B	2
AUBIGNAC	122	2	C	4
L'AUMONE (Petit Cîteaux)	123	3	C-G	1
AUNAY	124	3	C-B	2
BALERNE	125	4	B	2
BARBEAUX	126	2	B-M	2
BARBERY	127	3	C-B	2
BARZELLE	128	2	C	2
BAUMGARTEN	129	4	R-C	2
BEAUBEC	130	2	C-G	1
BEAUGERAIS	131	2	C-I	4
BEAULIEU-en-BASSIGNY	132	4	B	2
BEAUPRE	133	4	B	2
BEAUPRE	134	4	B	2
BEGARD	135	5	B	3
BELLAIGUE*	136	6	C	4
BELLE-EAU (Belleau)	137	3	C	2
BELLEBRANCHE	138	2	C	2
BELLEPERCHE	139	4	C-B	4
BELLEVAUX	140	4	C-B	2
BELLOC (Beaulieu-en-Rouergue)*	141	5	C-G-B	5
La BENISSON-DIEU	142	6	C-G	5
La BENISSON-DIEU (Nizors)	143	4	G-B	2
BERDOUES	144	4	C-B	2
Les BERNARDINS	145	4	C-G	1
Le BEUIL	146	2	C	4
BITHAINE	147	4	C-B	1
BOHERIES	148	4	B	2
BOIS-GROLAND	149	4	R-B	2
La BOISSIERE*	150	4	C-B	3
BONLIEU (Carbon-Blanc)	151	4	C-G-B	2
BONLIEU	152	3	C	2
BONNE-AIGUE (Bonaygue)	153	4	C-B	2
BONNECOMBE*	154	6	C-G	4
BONNEFONT-en-COMMINGES (Cloister in Cloisters, N.Y.)	155	3	C-G	5

Abbey	Map Ref.	Condition	Style	Accessibility
BONNEFONTAINE*	156	3	C	2
BONNEVAL*	157	6	C-G-M	2
BONNEVAUX	158	1	C	2
BONNEVAUX	159	4	C-G-B	1
BONPORT*	160	4	C	3
BON-REPOS	161	3	C-G-B	5
BOQUEN*	162	6	C-G	5
Le BOUCHET (Vauluisant)	163	2	C	2
BOUILLAS	164	2	C	4
BOULANCOURT	165	1	—	2
BOULBONNE	166	4	B	2
BOURAS	167	3	C	2
BOUSCHAUD*	168	4	C	4
BREUIL-BENOIT	169	6	C-G-B	0
BULLION	170	3	C	4
La BUSSIERE*	171	6	C-G	5
BUZAY	172	3	B	2
CADOUIN*	173	6	C-G	5
CALERS-en-FOIX	174	2	C	4
CANDEIL (La Bessière)	175	1	—	4
CARNOET (St. Maurice)	176	4	C-G	5
CERCAMP	177	4	B-C	1
CERCANCEAUX	178	4	C	1
CHAALIS	179	4	G-B	5
La CHALADE	180	6	G	5
CHALIVOY	181	2	B	1
CHALOCHE	182	4	C-B	3
Les CHAMBONS	183	2	C	4
CHAMPAGNE	184	4	C	5
La CHARITE	185	4	C-M	2
La CHARITE-lès-LEZINNES	186	1	C	1
La CHARMOYE	187	4	B	2
CHARON	188	1	—	2
La CHASSAGNE-en-BRESSE	189	2	G-B	2
Les CHATELLIERS (Ilderé)	190	3	C	4
Les CHATELLIERS	191	3	G	1
CHATILLON	192	1	—	4
CHEHERY (Chéri)	193	5	B	1

Abbey	Map Ref.	Con- dition	Style	Accessi- bility
CHEMINON	194	2	C-G	2
CHERLIEU	195	3	C-B	2
CHEZERY	196	2	B	4
CITEAUX	197	6	G-B-M	2
CLAIREFONTAINE	198	4	B	2
CLAIRLIEU	199	2	C	2
CLAIRMARAIS	200	2	G	4
CLAIRMONT (Clermont)*	201	4	C	5
CLAIRVAUX	202	4	C-B	3
La CLARTE-DIEU	203	4	C-G-B	2
COETMALOEN	204	3	B	4
La COLOMBE	205	2	C	4
La COUR-DIEU	206	4	C-G	2
La CRETE	207	3	G	2
DALON	208	4	C-B	2
EAUNES*	209	6	G-B-M	2
Les ECHARLIS	210	4	G-B	2
ELAN	211	6	C-I-B	4
L'EPAU*	212	5	C-G	5
L'ESCALADIEU*	213	5	C	5
ESCUREY	214	4	C-B	2
L'ESTREE	215	2	C-B	1
L'ETOILE*	216	5	C	3
La FAISE	217	4	C-I-B	2
FENIERS (Val-Honeste)	218	4	C-G	4
La FERTE	219	4	B	1
Les FEUILLANTS	220	2	C	2
FLARAN*	221	5	C	5
FOIGNY	222	2	C-M	4
FONTAINE-DANIEL	223	4	C-B	3
FONTAINEJEAN-en-GATINAIS*	224	3	C	2
FONTAINE-les-BLANCHES (Les Alleux)	225	2	C	2
FONTENAY**	226	5	C	5
FONTFROIDE*	227	5	C	5
FONT GUILLEM	228	4	C-B	2
FONTMORIGNY*	229	5	C	3
FOUCARMONT	230	2	B	1

Abbey	Map Ref.	Con- dition	Style	Accessi- bility
FRANQUEVAUX	231	2	C	1
FREISTROFF	232	1	B	1
La FRENADE	233	3	C-B	2
FROIDMONT	234	2	C	2
Le GARD	235	6	B	2
La GARDE-DIEU	236	4	C-G-B	2
GIMONT (Planselve)				
(Door in Cloisters, N.Y.)	237	4	C-G	4
GONDOM	238	4	C	2
GOURDON (Abbaye Nouvelle)	239	3	C-G	4
La GRACE-DIEU	240	6	C-B	2
La GRACE-DIEU	241	4	C	2
GRANDSELVE	242	2	B	1
GROSBOIS (Grosbot, Font-Vive)	243	3	C-B	2
HAUTECOMBE	244	6	C-I-B-M	5
HAUTE-FONTAINE	245	3	C-B	1
HAUTESEILLE	246	3	C	2
IGNY	247	6	M	3
L'ISLE-DIEU I	748	1	—	4
L'ISLE-DIEU II				
(La Blanche, Noirmoutier)	248	3	G-B	1
L'ISLE-en-BARROIS	249	2	C-B	2
Le JAU	250	3	C	4
JOUY-en-BRIE	251	3	C	2
LANDAIS	252	3	C	5
LANGONNET	253	6	C-M-B	5
LANNOY	254	4	C-B	2
LANVAUX	255	2	C-B	3
LARRIVOUR	256	1	C	1
LEONCEL*	257	6	C	4
LIEU-CROISSANT (Les Trois Rois)	258	2	C	4
LIEU-DIEU-en-PONTHIEU	259	4	B	4
LOC-DIEU*	260	6	C-G-M	5
LONGPONT*	261	4	G-B	5
LONGUAY	262	4	C-G	2
LONGVILLIERS	263	1	C	2
LOOS	264	4	B	1
Le LOROUX	265	3	C-G	3

Abbey	Map Ref.	Con- dition	Style	Accessi- bility
LORROY	266	3	C-B	2
LUCELLE	749	4	C	4
MAIZIERES	267	4	B	2
MARCILLY	268	3	C	0
MAZAN	269	3	C-G	4
MELLERAY*	270	6	C-B	5
La MERCI-DIEU	271	3	C-B	2
Le MIROIR	272	3	C	4
MONTIER-en-ARGONNE	273	2	C-M	1
MONTPEYROUX	274	3	C-B	2
MONT-Ste MARIE	275	2	C-M	1
MOREILLES	276	2	B	4
MORES	277	2	C	4
MORIMOND	278	2	C-B	4
MORTEMER*	279	4	C-B	5
NEUBOURG (Neuburg)	280	1	B	2
La NOE	281	2	C	4
NOIRLAC*	282	5	C	5
OBAZINE*	283	6	C	5
OLIVET	284	4	G-B	2
OURSCAMP*	285	6	C-B	5
PAIRIS	286	3	C-B	2
PALAIS-NOTRE-DAME	287	2	C	2
PERSEIGNE	288	3	C	1
PEYRIGNAC	289	2	C	1
La PEYROUSE	290	2	R	4
Les PIERRES	291	2	C	4
PIETE-DIEU	292	1	C	4
Le PIN	293	4	C-G-B	4
PONTAUT (mostly in Cloisters, N.Y.)	294	4	C	2
PONTIFROID	295	6	G-B	4
PONTIGNY*	296	6	C	5
PONTROND	297	2	I	4
PRE-BENOIT	298	3	C-B	4
La PREE	299	6	C-G-B	3
PREUILLY*	300	4	C	4
PRIERES	301	6	M	1
QUINCY	302	4	C-I	1

Abbey	Map Ref.	Con- dition	Style	Accessi- bility
Le RECLUS	303	4	C	2
REIGNY	304	4	C	0
Le RELECQ*	305	6	C-G	4
Le RIVET	306	6	C-M	0
Les ROCHES	307	2	G	2
ROSIERES	308	2	C-B	2
ROYAUMONT*	309	4	C-G	5
St ANDRE-de-GOUFFERN	310	3	C-G	4
St AUBIN-des-BOIS	311	3	C-G	2
St BENOIT-en-WOEVRE	312	2	B	4
St JEAN d'AULPS*	313	3	C	4
St LEONARD-des-CHAUMES	314	1	—	4
St MARCEL	315	2	M	2
St SULPICE-en-BUGEY	316	2	C	2
SAUVELADE*	317	6	R-I	4
SAUVEREAL	318	2	—	4
SAVIGNY	319	3	C	4
Les SELLIERES	320	2	M	0
SENANQUE*	321	6	C	5
SEPT-FONS	322	6	B	1
SIGNY	323	1	—	2
SILVACANE*	324	5	C	5
SILVANES*	325	6	C	5
STURZELBRONN	326	6	B	4
TAMIE (old abbey)	327	2	C	4
THEULEY	328	2	C-B	2
Le THORONET*	329	5	C	5
TIRONNEAU	330	1	—	4
TORIGNY	331	1	—	4
La TRAPPE	332	6	C-B-M	2
TRISAIE	333	3	C-B	2
TROIS-FONTAINES*	334	4	C-B	4
ULMET	749	2	C	4
Le VAL*	335	4	C-B	3
Le VALASSE	336	4	C-B-M	5
VAL-BENOITE	337	4	C-G-B	2
VALBONNE	338	3	C	1
VALCROISSANT*	339	4	C	2

Abbey	Map Ref.	Con-dition	Style	Accessi-bility
VALENCE	340	4	C	1
La VALETTE	341	2	C	4
VALLOIRES	342	6	B	5
VALMAGNE*	343	5	G	5
Le VAL-RICHER	344	4	B	1
VALROY	345	1	C	2
VALSAINTES	346	3	C	2
VARENNES	347	6	C-B	4
VAUCELLES*	348	4	C	5
VAUCLAIR	349	3	C	4
VAULUISANT	350	4	C-I-B	4
Les VAUX-DE-CERNAY*	351	4	C-M	5
VAUX-EN-ORNOIS	352	2	B-M	1
VAUX-LA-DOUCE	353	2	C	2
La VIEUXVILLE	354	4	C-B	1
VILLELONGUE*	355	4	C	4
La VILLENEUVE	356	3	B	5
VILLERS-BETNACH (Weilersbetnach)	357	2	C	1
Les BLANCHES (Abbaye Blanche)*	V	6	C	5
FONTAINE-GUÉRARD*	VI	4	C-G	5
LIEU (Lieu-l'Abbaye)	VII	5	C	2
Le LYS*	VIII	3	C	4
MAUBUISSON (Notre Dame La Royale)*	IX	4	C	5
RIEUNETTE*	X	6	C	3
VIGNOGOUL*	XI	6	G	2
Le CLOS VOUGEOT*	B	5	C-I	5
FONTCALVY*	C	4	C	4
GILLY-lès-CITEAUX	D	5	C	4
VILLERON (Vaulaurent)*	E	5	C	1

GERMANY (map p. 224)

Abbey	Map Ref.	Con-dition	Style	Accessi-bility
ALDERSBACH	358	6	B	4
ALTENBERG*	359	6	G	5
ALTZELLE	360	3	C	2

Abbey	Map Ref.	Con- dition	Style	Accessi- bility
AMELUNXBORN*	361	6	C	4
ARNSBURG*	362	4	C	5
BEBENHAUSEN*	363	5	C-G	5
BILDHAUSEN	364	6	B	2
BREDELAR	365	5	B	1
BRONNBACH*	366	6	C-B	4
BUCH (Ilgental)	367	3	C	4
CAMP (Altenkamp)*	368	6	G-B	5
CHORIN*	369	4	C-G	5
DARGUN*	370	6	C-B	4
DERNEBURG	371	4	R-B-M	1
DISIBODENBERG	372	3	R-C	4
DOBERAN*	373	6	G	4
DOBRILUGK	374	6	G	4
EBERBACH*	375	5	C	5
EBRACH*	376	6	C-G-B	2
ELDENA	377	3	C-G	4
EUSSERTHAL*	378	6	C	4
FÜRSTENFELD	379	6	B	4
FÜRSTENZELL	380	6	B	4
GEORGENTHAL	381	3	C-G	4
GOTTESZELL	382	6	B	4
GRÜNHAIN	383	1	—	4
HAINA*	384	5	C-G	3
HARDEHAUSEN	385	4	B-M	2
HEILSBRONN*	386	6	R-C-G	4
HEISTERBACH*	387	3	R-C-B	4
HERRENALB	388	3	C	4
HIDDENSEE	389	1	—	4
HIMMELPFORTE	390	4	G	4
HIMMEROD*	391	6	C-G-B	4
HÜDE*	392	3	C-G	4
IHLO	393	1	—	4
KAISHEIM*	394	6	G	4
KÖNIGSBRONN	395	2	G-B	4
LANGHEIM	396	2	B	4
LEHNIN*	397	6	C	4
LOCCUM*	398	6	C-G-B	5

Abbey	Map Ref.	Con- dition	Style	Accessi- bility
MARIENFELD*	399	6	C-G-B	4
MARIENRODE (Backenrode)	400	6	G-B	4
MARIENSTATT*	401	6	C-G-B	3
MARIENTAL*	402	6	C	4
MAULBRONN*	403	6	C-G	5
MICHAELSTEIN	404	3	C-B	5
NEUENKAMP	405	1	—	4
NEUZELLE	406	6	G-B	3
OTTERBERG*	407	6	C-G	4
PFORTA (Schulpforta)	408	6	R-C-G	5
RAITENHASLACH	409	6	B	4
REIFENSTEIN	410	5	B	1
REINFELD	411	1	—	4
RIDDAGSHAUSEN*	412	6	C	5
RUHEKLOSTER (Ryd) (Schloß Glücksburg)	413	2	—	5
SALEM*	414	6	G-(B)	4
SCHARNEBECK (Marienbach)	415	4	B	2
SCHÖNAU	416	4	G	4
SCHÖNTHAL	417	6	B-(G)	4
SITTICHENBACH (Sichem)	418	1	—	4
STOLPE	420	1	—	4
TENNENBACH (gate-chapel only)	421	4	G	3
TENNENBACH (rebuilt as Ludwigskirch)	421a	6	M	4
VIERZEHNHEILIGEN	422	6	B	4
VOLKENRODE	423	6	C	4
WALDERBACH*	424	6	C-B	4
WALDSASSEN	425	6	B	4
WALKENRIED*	426	4	C-G	5
WÖRSCHWEILER	427	3	C-G	5
ZINNA*	428	6	C	4
HOVEN (Marienborn)	XII	6	R-C	3
ISENHAGEN*	XIII	6	C-G	3
St THOMAS an der KYLL*	XIV	6	C-B	3
SELIGENTHAL	XV	6	G-B	4
WIENHAUSEN*	XVI	6	G-I-B	3

Abbey	Map Ref.	Con- dition	Style	Accessi- bility
GREECE (map p. 230)				
CHORTAITON	429			
DAPHNI*	430	6	Byzantine-C	5
GERGERI	431	0	—	—
S. MARIA VARANGIORUM	432	0	—	—
ZARAKA	433	2	G	4
HOLLAND (map p. 227)				
ADUARD (infirmary only)*	434	6	C-G	4
BLOEMKAMP (Oldekleaster)	435	I	—	4
EITEREN (Marienberg)	436			
GERKESKLEASTER (Jerusalem)	437	2	G	4
KLAARKAMP	438	I	C	4
MARIENKROON	439	I	—	4
MENTERNA	440	I	—	4
TERMUNTEN (Menterna II)*	440a	6	G	4
ROERMOND	XVII	6	C-G	5
KLOOSTERZANDE	F	6	C-G	3
HUNGARY (map p. 223)				
BELAPATFALVA (Bel-Harom-Kuti)*	441	6	C	4
CZIKADOR	442			
ERCSI	443	I	—	4
KERESZTUR (Sancta Crux, Vertheskerestur)	444	3	R-C	4
PAZTO	445	2	C	4
PILIS	446	2	C	4
PORNO	447	I	—	4
SZENTGOTTHARD	448	6	C-B	4
ZIRC I	449	2	C	4
ZIRC II	449a	6	B	4
IRELAND (map p. 220)				
ABINGTON (Owney)	450	I	—	4
ASSAROE	451	2	C	4
BALTINGLASS*	452	3	C	5

Abbey	Map Ref.	Con-dition	Style	Accessi-bility
BECTIVE*	453	4	G	5
BOYLE*	454	4	C-G	5
CLARE	455	5	G	4
COMBER	456	I	—	4
CORCOMROE*	457	3	C	4
Abbey DORNEY	458	3	G	4
DUNBRODY*	459	4	C	5
Abbey FEALE	460	I	—	4
FERMOY	461	I	—	4
GLANRAGH (Glanawydan)	462	I	—	4
GRAIGUENAMANAGH (Duiske)	463	6	C-G	5
GREY*	464	3	C-G	5
HOLY CROSS*	465	6	C-G	5
HORE*	466	3	C-G	5
INCH*	467	3	C	5
INISHLOUNAGHT	468	2	R-C	4
JERPOINT*	469	4	C-G	5
KILBEGGAN	470	I	—	4
KILCOOLY*	471	4	C-G	5
KILLENNY	472	I	—	4
Abbey KNOCKMOY*	473	3	C	4
Abbey LARA	474	3	C	4
Abbey LEIX	475	I	—	4
MACOSQUIN	476	I	C	4
Abbey MAHON	477	2	C	4
MELLIFONT*	478	4	C-G	5
MIDLETON	479	I	—	4
MONASTERANENAGH	480	3	C-G	4
MONASTEREVIN	481	I	—	2
NEWRY	482	I	—	4
St MARY'S DUBLIN *(chapter house only)*	483	4	C	3
Abbey SHRULE	484	2	C	4
Abbey STRAWLEY	485	I	—	4
TINTERN MINOR*	486	4	C-G	5
TRACTON	487	I	—	4

Abbey	Map Ref.	Con-dition	Style	Accessi-bility
ITALY (map p. 229)				
ACQUAFREDDA	488	6	R-B	4
ACQUAFORMOSA	489	1	—	4
ACQUALUNGA	490	6	C-G	4
ALTOFONTE	491	6	B	4
BADIA a SETTIMO*	492	6	R-C-G-I-B	3
BADIA CERRETO*	493	6	C	4
BADIA S. SALVATORE	494	6	R-I	5
BARONA	495	1	—	4
BRONDOLO	496	1	B	4
BUONSOLLAZZO	497	6	B	4
CABUABBAS (S. Maria di Corte)*	498	3	C	4
CAPOLAGO	499	6	C-B-M	4
CASAMARI*	500	6	C	5
CASALVOLONE	501	1	—	4
CASANOVA d'ABRUZZO	502	2	C	4
CASANOVA TORINESE	503	6	C-B	5
CAVA TIGOZZI	504	6	B	4
CHIARAVALLE d'ANCONA*	505	6	C-B	4
CHIARAVALLE della COLOMBA*	506	6	C-B	5
CHIARAVALLE di FIASTRA*	507	6	C-I-B	4
CHIARAVALLE MILANESE*	508	6	C-G-B	5
CORAZZO	509	3	C	4
FALLERI*	510	4	R-C	4
La FERRARIA	511	3	C	4
FOLLINA (Sanavalle)*	512	6	R-C-I	5
FONTEVIVO*	513	6	C	4
FOSSANOVA*	514	6	C	5
LUCEDIO	515	5	C-B	1
MARMOSOLIO	516	1	—	4
MATINA*	517	4	C	2
MIRTETO	518	4	R	4
MONTECORONA	519	6	R-C-B	4
MONTEFAVALE	520	1	—	4
Basilica di MONTE MURGO*	521	3	C-G	4
MORIMONDO CORONATO*	522	6	C	4
NOVARA di SICILIA	523	6	G-B	4
L'OSPEDALE del PIAVE	524	1	—	4

Abbey	Map Ref.	Con-dition	Style	Accessi-bility
PALAZZOLO	525	6	R-B	2
PREALLO (S. Maria del Porale)	526	1	—	4
QUARTAZZOLA	527	5	B	0
QUARTO	528	4	C	1
REALVALLE	529	2	C-G	1
RIPALTA di PUGLIA	530	6	C	2
RIVALTA di TORINO	531	5	B	1
RIVALTA SCRIVIA*	532	6	C-B	4
ROCCADIA	533	1	—	4
ROCCAMADORE	534	1	—	4
SAGITTARIO	535	2	C	4
SALA	536	3	R	4
SAMBUCINA*	537	6	C-I	4
S. AGOSTINO di MONTALTO	538	2	R	1
S. ANDREA di SESTRI	539	6	R-G	1
S. ANGELO in FRIGIDO	540	2	R	4
S. BENEDETTO al SUBASIO	541	6	R	2
S. FREDIANO (S. Friano)	542	1	—	0
S. GALGANO*	543	4	C	5
S. GIOVANNI in LAMIS	544	6	I-B	4
S. GIULIANO al MONTE	545	6	R	4
S. GIUSTO di TUSCANIA	546	5	R	0
S. GODENZO	547	6	R	5
S. MARIA ARABONA*	548	6	C	4
S. MARIA de CARITATE (de Sylva)	549	0	—	—
S. MARIA del GALESO	550	6	C	2
S. MARIA dell'ARCO	551	1	—	4
S. MARIA dell'ARCO II	551a	6	B	4
S. MARIA della VITTORIA	552	2	C	4
S. MARIA delle PALUDI (S. Maria de Paulis)	553	3	C	4
S. MARIA delle TERRATE	554	1	—	4
S. MARIA dell'INCORONATA	555	6	M	5
S. MARIA dello ZERBINO	556	—	—	—
S. MARIA di PONZA	557	1	—	4
S. MARIA in STRADA	558	6	C-B	5
S. MARTINO al CIMINO*	559	6	C	5
S. MICHELE alla VERRUCA	560	2	R	4

Abbey	Map Ref.	Con- dition	Style	Accessi- bility
S. Nicola di Agrigento*	561	6	C-G	4
S. Pantaleone a Monte Faeta	562	1	R	2
S. Pastore	563	3	C	0
S. Pietro alla Canonica	564	6	G-B	4
S. Pietro a Paliano	565	6	I	4
S. Pietro di Ferentillo	566	5	R	5
S. Sebastiano ad Catacumbas	567	6	B	5
S. Severo	568	2	R	2
S. Spirito della Valle	569	0	—	—
S. Spirito del Vespro*	570	6	C	4
S. Spirito di Zannone	571	2	C	4
S. Spirito di Zannone II	571a	3	C-G	0
S. Spirito d'Ocre*	572	5	G	3
S. Stefano del Bosco	573	6	B	5
S. Stefano del Corno	574	1	—	1
S. Tommaso del Borgognoni	575	1	—	1
SS. Trinita' del Legno	576	2	R	4
SS. Trinita' di Palermo (La Magione)*	577	6	C	4
SS. Vito & Salvo	578	1	—	2
Spano'	579	2	G	1
Staffarda*	580	6	C	5
Sterpeto	581	6	M	4
Tiglieto*	582	5	C	1
Le Tre Fontane*	583	6	C	5
Valserena (S. Martino de' Bocci)*	584	5	C	2
Valvisciolo*	585	6	C	4
S. Maria della Valle (Badiazza)	XVIII	3	C	4
Valle Christi*	XIX	3	C	4

LATVIA (map p. 228)

Dünamünde	725	2	G	1

LEBANON (map p. 230)

Belmont (Dayr Balamand)*	586	6	C-G	3

Abbey	Map Ref.	Con- dition	Style	Accessi- bility
NORWAY (map p. 228)				
Hovedø	587	2	C	4
Lyse Kloster*	588	2	R-C	4
Tuterø (Tautra)	589	1	—	4
POLAND (map p. 223)				
Bierzwnik	590	6	G	4
Bledzew (Blesen, Neu Dobrilugk)	591	1	—	4
Bukowo (Buckow)	592	6	G	4
Henrykow (Heinrichau)	593	6	C-B	4
Imielnica (Himmelwitz, Chelmnick)	594	6	G	4
Jedrzejow (Andreovia)*	595	4	C-B	4
Kamieniec (Kamenz) (Zabkowicki)	596	6	G-B	4
Kolbacz (Kolbatz)*	597	6	C-G-B	4
Koprzywnica*	598	6	C-B	4
Koronowo (Crone, Bessow)	599	6	G-B	4
Krzeszow (Grüßau)	600	6	B	5
Ląd*	601	6	B	4
Lubiaz (Leubus)*	602	6	G-B	2
Mironice (Himmelstätt)	603			
Mogila*	604	6	C-M	4
Obra	605	6	B	4
Oliwa	606	6	G-B	5
Paradyz (Paradies)	607	6	G-B	4
Pelplin (Neu Doberan)*	608	6	G	4
Przemet	609	6	R-B	4
Rudy (Rauden)*	610	6	C-G-B	5
Sulejow*	611	4	C	5
Szczyrzyc*	612	6	R-C	3
Wąchock*	613	6	C-B	3
Wagrowiec (Leknow)	614	6	G-B	2
Trzebnica*	xx	6	C-G-B	4

Abbey	Map Ref.	Condition	Style	Accessibility
PORTUGAL (map p. 226)				
AGUIAR	615	6	C	4
ALCOBAÇA*	616	5	C	5
BOURO	617	4	C-I-B	3
ERMELO	618	6	R-G-B	4
ESTRELA (Maceira de Covelliana)	619			
FIÃES	620	6	C-I	4
FRADES (Almaziva) (S. Paulo de Coimbra)	621			
JUNHAS (Pitões)*	622	6	R-C-B	4
LAFÕES	623	2	B	2
MACEIRA DÃO	624	3	B	2
SALZEDAS	625	6	C-B	4
S. JOÃO de TAROUCA*	626	6	C-B	4
S. PEDRO das AGUIAS	627	6	B	I
SEIÇA	628	2	C	2
SEVER	629			
TAMARÃES	630	I	—	4
CELAS	XXI	6	R-I-B	5
LORVÃO	XXII	5	R-B	2
ROMANIA (map p. 223)				
EGRES	631	2	C	0
KERZ (Cirta)	632	4	C	4
SCOTLAND (map p. 220)				
BALMERINO	633	2	C	4
COUPAR ANGUS	634	6	G	4
CULROSS*	635	6	G	4
DEER	636	3	C	5
DUNDRENNAN*	637	3	C-G	5
GLENLUCE*	638	3	C-G	5
KINLOSS	639	2	C-G	4
MELROSE*	640	4	G	5
NEWBATTLE	641	2	G	2
SADDELL	642	2	C	4
SWEETHEART (New Abbey)*	643	4	C-G	5

Abbey	Map Ref.	Con- dition	Style	Accessi- bility
ISLE OF MAN (map p. 220)				
RUSHEN	644	2	C-G	4
SLOVAKIA (map p. 223)				
SZEPES (Zips)	36	1	—	4
SLOVENIA (map p. 222)				
KOSTANJEVICA (Landstrass)*	743	6	C-B	3
STIČNA (Sittich)*	744	6	C-B	4
SPAIN (map p. 226)				
ACIBEIRO	645	6	R	4
ARMENTERA	419	6	C	4
La BAIX	646	4	R	4
BELMONTE	647	2	C	1
BENAVIDES (Valverde)	648			
BENIFAÇAR	649	4	C-G	4
BONAVAL	650	3	C	4
BUJEDO de JUARROS	651	6	C-B	4
CARRACEDO	652	4	C-I-B	4
CASTAÑEDA	653	6	R-I	4
ESCARP	654	2	C-B	1
La ESPINA*	655	5	C-I-B	5
FITERO*	656	6	C-I	4
FRANQUERA	657			
GUMIEL	658			
HERRERA (Saya, Sajazarra)	659			
HUERTA*	660	6	C-I-B	5
IRANZU*	661	6	C	5
JUNQUEIRA	662	6	C	4
LEYRE*	663	6	R-C-M	5
MATALLANA	664	3	C	4
MEIRA	665	6	C-I	4
MELON	666	4	C-I	4
MONFERO	667	6	B	4
MONSALUD de CORCOLES	668	4	C-I	4
MONTEDERRAMO	669	6	C-G-I	4
MORERUELA*	670	4	C	5

Abbey	Map Ref.	Con- dition	Style	Accessi- bility
NOGALES	671			
La OLIVA*	672	6	C-G	5
OSERA*	673	6	C-G-B	2
OVILA	674	4	C-I	4
OYA*	675	6	C-I-B	4
PALAZUELOS	676	6	C-B	4
PEÑAMAYOR	677	6	C	4
PIEDRA	678	4	C-M	4
POBLET*	679	6	C-G	5
RIO SECO	680			
RUEDA de EBRO*	681	5	C-G	5
SACRAMENIA (refectory, cloister in Miami, Fl.)	682	6	C-G	4
SANDOVAL	683	6	C-G-B	3
SANTA FE' (Fuenclara)	684			
SANTA FE' II	684a	3	B	I
S. CLODIO DE RIBADAVIA	748	6	C	4
SANTES CREUS*	685	5	C-G-I	5
S. MARIA la REAL (La Granja)	686	2	C-B	5
S. MARIA de la GLORIA	687	6	B	4
S. ISIDORO del CAMPO	688	6	G-I	5
SOBRADO de los MONJES	689	6	C-G-I-B	5
SOTOSALBOS (Sta Maria de la Sierra)	690	3	C	4
VALBUENA de DUERO*	691	6	C-G	5
VALDEDIOS*	692	6	R-C-I	5
VALDEIGLESIAS	693	3	C-G	4
VALDIGNA	694	4	C-G	5
VALPARAISO	695	I	—	4
La VEGA	696	6	C-G	5
VERUELA*	697	5	C-G	5
VILLANUEVA de OSCOS	698			
GRADEFES*	XXIII	6	C	2
LAS HUELGAS*	XXIV	6	R-C-G-B	5
S. ANDRES del ARROYO	XXV	6	R-C	2

Abbey	Map Ref.	Con- dition	Style	Accessi- bility
SWEDEN (map p. 228)				
ALVASTRA*	699	3	C	5
ÅS	700	1	—	4
GUDSBERGA	701			
HERREVAD	702	2	C	4
JULITA (Saba) (Julita Castle on site)	703	2	G-R-B	5
NYDALA*	704	4	C	4
ROMA (Gudvala)*	705	3	C	5
VARNHEM*	706	6	C	4
GUDHEM	XXVI	3	C	4
VRETAKLOSTER*	XXVII	6	C	5
SWITZERLAND (map p. 225)				
BONMONT*	707	5	C	2
HAUTCRET	708	1	—	1
HAUTERIVE*	709	6	C-G-B	5
FRIENISBERG	710	2	C	2
KAPPEL*	711	5	G	4
MONTHERON	712	2	C	4
SANKT URBAN	713	6	B	4
WETTINGEN*	714	5	C-G-B	2
La MAIGRAUGE*	XXVIII	6	C	2
SYRIA (map p. 230)				
SALVATIO	715	0	—	—
St JEAN-au-BOIS	716	0	—	—
St SERGIUS	717	0	—	—
Ste TRINITE-de-REFESCH	718	0	—	—
TURKEY (map p. 230)				
LAURUS	719	0	—	—
S. ANGELUS in PETRA	720	0	—	—
S. ANGELUS de RUFINIANO	721	0	—	—
S. FOCA	722	0	—	—
S. GEORGES de JUBINO	723	0	—	—
S. STEPHANUS de GRECIA	724	0	—	—

Abbey	Map Ref.	Con- dition	Style	Accessi- bility
WALES (map p. 220)				
ABERCONWY	728	6	C	4
BASINGWERK*	729	3	C	5
CWMHIR	730	1	C-G	4
CYMMER	731	2	G	5
LLANTARNAM	732	1	G	2
MAENAN	733	1	—	4
MARGAM*	734	6	R-C	5
NEATH*	735	4	C-G	5
STRATA FLORIDA	736	2	R-C	5
STRATA MARCELLA	737	1	—	4
TINTERN*	738	4	G	5
VALLE CRUCIS*	739	4	C-G	5
WHITLAND	740	1	—	4
YUGOSLAVIA (Serbia) (map p. 222)				
ABRAHAM (Bacs Monostor)	741	1	—	4
BELAKUT (Petervarad)	742	1	—	4

THE BRITISH ISLES

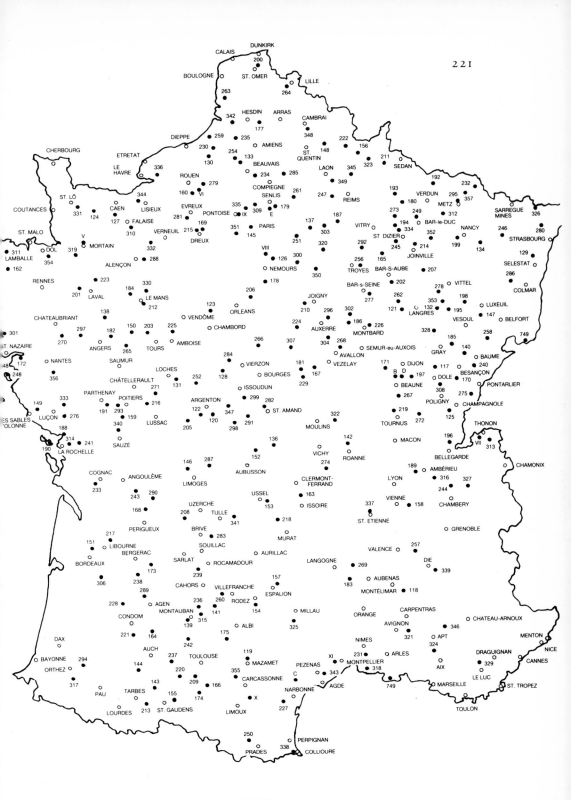

FRANCE

SLOVENIA

MARIBOR

744
LJUBLJANA ● 743
NOVO
MESTO

747

ZAGREB

POSTOJNA

CROATIA

KARLOVAC

VELIKA 746

OSIJEK

741

NOVI SAD

742

RIJEKA

745
GLINA

SLAVONSKI BROD

BELGRADE

POLA

BOSNIA-
HERZEGOVINA

SERBIA

ZADAR

TROGIR
SPLIT

SARAJEVO

MOSTAR

MONTENEGRO

DUBROVNIK

THE BALKANS

EASTERN EUROPE

FLENSBURG ● 413

389 ●

● KIEL

373 STRALSUND ●
ROSTOCK 405 ● 377 ●
WISMAR 370 DEMMIN ●
411 ● 420 ●
● LUBECK

SCHWERIN ○ NEUBRANDENBURG

● HAMBURG

393 ● OLDENBURG ● 415 390 ●
○ 392 LUNEBURG 369 ●
BREMEN EBERSWALDE ○

CELLE ● XIII
NIENBURG ○ ● XVI BERLIN ○
398 ● HANNOVER BRANDENBURG ○ POTSDAM ● 397
HAMELIN ○ 400 ● BRUNSWICK ● 402 EISENHUTTENSTADT ○ ● 406
MUNSTER ○ 399 ● 371 ● 412 MAGDEBURG ○ 428 ●
361 ● 404 ● HERZBERG ○
PADERBORN ○ 426 374 ●
DORTMUND ○ ● 385 GÖTTINGEN ○ 418 ○ HALLE TORGAU ○
368 ● ○ ESSEN ● 365 410 ● 423 LEIPZIG ○ 360 ● MEISSEN
DUSSELDORF ○ 384 ● KASSEL ○ MUHLHAUSEN ○ 408 ● 367 ● DRESDEN
359 ● SIEGEN GOTHA WEIMAR
○ COLOGNE ○ ○ MARBURG ERFURT ○ JENA
AACHEN ○ BONN 401 ● 381 ● ZWICKAU ○
XII ● 387 ● GIESSEN 383 ●
KOBLENZ WETZLAR ○ ○ FULDA
XIV ○ 362 ●
391 ● WIESBADEN ○ ● 364 LICHTENFELS
375 ● FRANKFURT BAD KISSINGEN 422 ● ● 396
MAINZ 376 ● 425 ○
372 ● 366 ● BAMBERG BAYREUTH
TRIER ○ WURZBURG
MANNHEIM
407 ● ○ ● 416 386 ●
KAISERSLAUTERN HEIDELBERG ● 417 NUREMBERG
SAARBRUCKEN ○ 427 ● 378 ● ANSBACH
PIRMASENS 424 ●
403 ● REGENSBURG ○ 382 ●
KARLSRUHE ○ PFORZHEIM 394 ● ○ DEGGENDORF
● 388 STUTTGART 395 ● INGOLSTADT ○ 358 ●
BADEN-BADEN ● 363 ○ 380 ● PASSAU
TUBINGEN LANDSHUT ○
421 ● ULM ○ XV ● ALTÖTTING
○● 421a AUGSBURG ○ 409 ●
FREIBURG 379 ● ○
SINGEN ○ 414 MUNICH
○ RAVENSBURG

GERMANY

PORRENTRUY

BÂLE

DELEMONT

BADEN
714

ZURICH

ST GALL

AARBURG

SOLOTHURN

BIEL

713

711

NEUCHATEL

710

BERNE

LUCERNE

SCHWUYZ

FRIBOURG
709

712

LAUSANNE

708
VEVEY

707
NYON

GENEVA

SWITZERLAND

THE IBERIAN PENINSULA

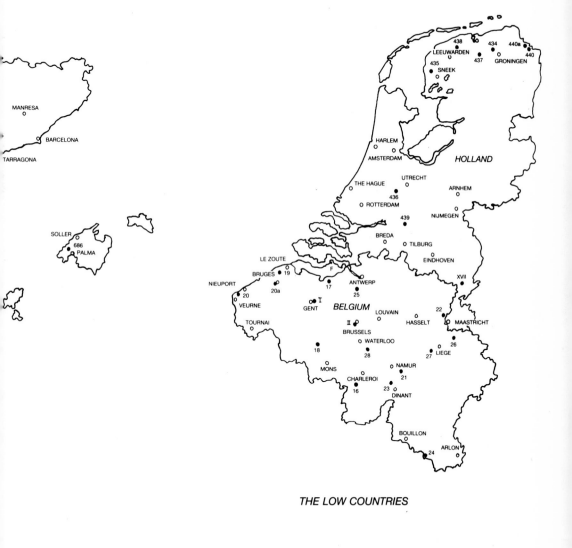

THE LOW COUNTRIES

SCANDINAVIA & THE BALTIC COUNTRIES

ITALY

12TH-CENTURY LATIN KINGDOM OF JERUSALEM – LATIN EMPIRE 13TH CENTURY

Appendix C
Staying in a Cistercian Abbey

In the hope that reading this book, or simply looking at the photographs, may awaken a desire in the reader to take a look at the abbeys for him or herself, I have prepared a list of establishments offering hospitality of one form or another to the tourist who wants to experience the added pleasure of actually dining and possibly sleeping where the white monks once lived and prayed.

The places I list below are no longer active Cistercian abbeys, but simply abbey buildings or even ruins where small and usually rustic guesthouses have been established. Though there are one or two luxury hotels, the average ex-abbey guesthouse is usually moderately priced, and much more atmospheric than an ordinary bed and breakfast (many are reputed to be haunted).

Rather than give prices, which would become out of date so quickly, I have indicated with a star system the price bracket into which each establishment falls. One star means cheap, two reasonable, three expensive to very expensive (but well worth it at least once in a lifetime). We shall certainly never forget the one night we spent at the hotel in the lay brothers' wing of the Vaux-de-Cernay near Paris – the atmosphere was unmatched by anything we have experienced before or since, the service absolutely exquisite in a charming 'olde worlde' sort of way, and the bill astronomical!

Most active Cistercian, and other, monasteries provide the wayfarer with some sort of hospitality. I have stayed at none of them and can offer no information concerning the facilities provided. I can only say that one day I turned up quite without warning at a convent of Cistercian nuns in Cortona to take some photographs (just before midday), and found a table laid and my lunch waiting for me when I had finished. Mother Abbess herself waited on me, and we engaged in stimulating conversation while I ate. The courses were four, the wine plentiful, and the coffee excellent. When I rose to leave and proffered payment, it was refused with a smile and the offer of an apple for my journey!

For ease of consultancy, in this appendix I have listed the abbeys by country, subdivided into regions. For each entry I have given the nearest town, the original name of the abbey, the current name of the establishment, the phone number if there is one, and the dining and sleeping facilities. Where a section is blank, the service described in that column is not provided or is irrelevant.

This list obviously reflects my personal experience and knowledge of the establishments listed, and makes no claim to be complete. As I visit more and more abbeys on my travels in Europe and the Near East, I hope to be able to add to it in future editions of this book.

Nearest town	Abbey	Current name	Telephone	Description	Dining Sleeping	

BELGIUM

ARDENNES
| Bouillon | ORVAL | Auberge à L'Ange Gardien | 061.311886 | in modern pub on site of medieval inn by gatehouse | D* | |

BRABANT
Brussels	VILLERS-la-VILLE	Hotel des Ruines	071.877057	in the 14th/19th c. abbey mill	D**	
Charleroi	AULNE	Caves de L'Abbaye	071.519828	in 17th c. undercroft	D*	
Charleroi	AULNE	Auberge de L'Abbaye	071.560195	in 13th c. mill	D**	

FLANDERS
| Bruges | TER DOEST | Hof Ter Doest | 050.544082 | in 17th c. buildings on site | D*** | |
| Coxyde | ABBAYE des DUNES | | | modern pub in the abbey ruins | | |

HERVE
| Liège | VAL-DIEU | Casse-Croute de L'Abbaye | | in abbey outbuildings | D* | |

DENMARK
| Tønder | LØGUMKLOSTER | | | open for Christmas holidays – board and lodging provided | D* | S* |

ENGLAND

CHESHIRE
| Chester | VALE ROYAL | The 16th–19th c. stately home on the abbey site is due to open as a country hotel | | | | |

GLOUCESTERSHIRE
| Tetbury | KINGSWOOD | Calcot Manor | 0166689.0391 | in the 15th c. abbey guest house | D** | S** |

OXFORDSHIRE
| Shipton-u-Wychwood | BRUERN | The Shaven Crown | 01993.830330 | in the 14th c. abbey guest house (pub food available) | D** | S** |

YORKSHIRE
| Ripon | JERVAULX | Jervaulx Hall | 01677.460235 | on the abbey site | D** | S** |

Nearest town	Abbey	Current name	Telephone	Description	Dining Sleeping	

FRANCE

ALSACE

| Porrentruy | LUCELLE | Maison de Vacances St Bernard | 89.40.85.38 | in updated medieval abbey outbuildings | D* | S* |

BERRY

| St Amand | NOIRLAC | Auberge de l'Abbaye | 48.96.22.58 | in the medieval gate-chapel | D** | |

BRITTANY

Nantes	VILLENEUVE	Hotel de l'Abbaye	40.04.40.25	in 18th c. abbey buildings	D**	S**
Pluvigner	LANVAUX		97.56.00.23	in 17th c. abbot's lodge		S*
Rostrenen	BON-REPOS	Hotellerie de l'Abbaye	96.24.98.38	in the medieval abbey stables	D**	S**

BURGUNDY

| Beaune | MAIZIERES | Chateau de Maizières | 85.49.45.79 | in 18th c. abbot's lodge | D** | S** |
| Chateauneuf | La BUSSIERE | | 80.49.02.29 | in the 13th/19th c. abbey | D* | S* |

CHAMPAGNE

| Brienne-le-Chateau | BOULANCOURT | Ferme Auberge | 25.04.60.18 | in a 19th c. building on the site | D* | S* |

GASCONY

| Bagnères-de-Bigorre | L'ESCALADIEU | | 62.39.13.13 | in 12th/17th c. abbey | D** | S** |

ILE-DE-FRANCE

| Rambouillet | VAUX-DE-CERNAY | | 01.34.85.23.00 | in the 13th/19th c. lay brother wing | D*** | S*** |

LIMOUSIN

| Boussac | PREBENOIT | Centre d'Animation et de Tourisme | 55.80.78.91 | in 12th/17th c. abbey ruins | D* | S* |

LANGUEDOC

| Montpellier | VALMAGNE | | 67.78.06.09 | 13th c. rooms available for functions | | |
| St Affrique | SILVANES | | 65.99.51.83 | in 12th c. dormitory and day room | D* | S* |

MAINE

| Le Mans | CHAMPAGNE | | 43.20.15.74 | in the 13th/17th c. lay brother wing | D* | S* |

NORMANDY

Bolbec	Le VALASSE		35.31.04.11	18th c. rooms available for functions		
Evreux	La NOÉ	Base de Loisirs	32.37.61.87	18th c. house on site (groups only)	D*	S*
Lyons-la-Forêt	MORTEMER		32.49.54.37	18th c. rooms available for functions		

Nearest town	Abbey	Current name	Telephone	Description	Dining Sleeping	
PICARDY						
Amiens	LE GARD		22.51.40.50	in 18th c. abbey buildings	D*	S*
Argoules	VALLOIRES		22.29.92.55	in 18th c. abbey buildings	D*	S*
Eu	LIEU-DIEU	Ecuries de Lieu-Dieu	22.30.92.23	in abbey stables	D*	S*
Soissons	LONGPONT		23.96.01.53	13th/18th c. rooms available for functions		
Soissons	LONGPONT	Hotel de l'Abbaye	23.96.02.44	within the 13th c. abbey precinct	D**	S**
PROVENCE						
Arles	SAUVERÉAL	Mas de Sylveréal	66.73.51.03	in 18th c. buildings on abbey site	D*	S*
Bollène	Le BOUCHET	Coopérative Viticole Abbaye du Bouchet	75.04.83.21	12th c. nuns' dormitory available for functions		
Gordes	SENANQUE		90.72.02.05	in 12th c. abbey	D*	S*
VENDÉE						
Luçon	MOREILLES		51.56.17.56	in 18th c. abbot's lodge	D*	S*

GERMANY

Nearest town	Abbey	Current name	Telephone	Description	Dining Sleeping	
BAVARIA						
Altötting	RAITENHASLACH		08677.7062	in former monastery	D**	S**
Vilshofen	ALDERSBACH	Gasthof Mayerhof	08543.1602	in the 13th c. abbey guesthouse	D**	S**
HESSEN						
Giessen	ARNSBURG	Alte Klostermühle	06404.2020	in 17th c. abbey mill	D**	S**
RHINELAND						
Cologne	ALTENBERG	Hotel Altenberger Hof	02174.4242	in 14th/19th c. abbey guesthouse	D**	S**
Mainz	EBERBACH		06723.4228	wine-tasting in the 13th c. infirmary		
Pforzheim	MAULBRONN	Klosterkeller	07043.6539	within the 13th c. abbey precinct	D**	
SWABIA						
Emmendingen	TENNENBACH	Gasthof 'Engel'	07641.8664	in the 16th c. abbey guesthouse	D*	S*
Herrenalb	BAD HERRENALB	Mönchs Posthotel	07083.7440	in modernised 14th c. guesthouse	D**	S**
WESTPHALIA						
Halle	MARIENFELD	Hotel Klostersforte	05247.7080	in baroque gatehouse	D**	S**

ITALY

Nearest town	Abbey	Current name	Telephone	Description	Dining Sleeping	
CAMPANIA						
Amalfi	S. PIETRO alla CANONICA	Hotel I Cappuccini	089.871008	in 12th/18th/19th c. abbey buildings	D***	S***
LAZIO						
Priverno	FOSSANOVA	Ristorante La Grancia	0773.93085	in the 13th c. barn	D**	
Soria	CASAMARI			in 12th c. precinct wall	D*	

Nearest town	Abbey	Current name	Telephone	Description	Dining Sleeping	
Viterbo	S. MARTINO al CIMINO			12th c. scriptorium available for functions		
MARCHE						
Macerata	FIASTRA			Wine tasting in the 12th c. lay brothers' refectory		
PIEDMONT						
Saluzzo	STAFFARDA	Locanda del Chiostro	0175.703108	in the 15th c. stables	D**	
TUSCANY						
Florence	BADIA a SETTIMO	Sig. Tanini	055.790007	12th c. cellarium available for functions. Pub/Bar in the 13th c. abbot's dining hall		
SPAIN						
ARAGON						
Zaragoza	PIEDRA	Hotel 'Monasterio de Piedra'	0976.849011	in the 12th/17th c. abbey buildings	D**	S**
SWITZERLAND						
GENEVA						
Geneva	BONMONT			in the 17th c. clubhouse (abbey now golf club)	D**	
LAUSANNE						
Lausanne	MONTHERON	Auberge de Montheron		in the 16th c. abbey guesthouse	D**	
ZURICH						
Baar (ZG)	KAPPEL	Wirtschaft zur Post	01.7641239	within the 14th c. abbey precinct	D**	
Wettingen	WETTINGEN	Gasthof Stemen	056.27.14.61	at abbey gates	D**	S**
WALES						
GWENT						
Chepstow	TINTERN	The Anchor Hotel	01291.689207	pub in 14th c. abbey outbuilding	D*	
GWYNEDD						
Llanrwst	CONWY	The Priory	01492.660247	19th c. hotel built with abbey stone	D**	S**
Llangollen	VALLE CRUCIS	Abbey Farm and camp site	01978.861297	in 18th c. farm on abbey site	D*	S*
ISLE OF MAN						
Ballasalla	RUSHEN	Abbey Hotel	01624.823240	19th c. hotel on abbey site	D**	S**

Notes

CHAPTER 3

1 Up until fairly recent times it was not considered necessary for a monk (i.e. a 'brother') who renounced the world to live in a religious community, also to become a priest (i.e. a 'father') empowered to say Mass and administer the Sacraments.

2 Due to the Black Death of 1348 and possibly the stronger appeal exercised on vocations from the humbler classes by the mendicant orders of Franciscans and Dominicans.

CHAPTER 4

1 *Mandé* in French, from which the English 'Maundy' is derived. Washing of the feet is still an important part of the Catholic ritual performed on Maundy Thursday.

CHAPTER 5

1 The Basilica del Murgo in Sicily is such a house, and the monks' advice was sought and expertise engaged in the building of Castel del Monte, that most enigmatic and breathtaking of castles in Apulia. Frederick also granted the monks of Morimondo in Lombardy authority over fishing, irrigation and navigation on the River Ticino.

2 As early as the 1220s, the Bavarian Abbey of Aldersbach was running Europe's first co-educational school, in an age when very few boys and no girls received any more than the rudiments of a formal education.

3 Of course this does not represent the Cistercians' first encounter with urban civilization. As early as the twelfth century many abbeys owned town houses where their farm produce could be stored for sale in the markets, their abbots could lodge while on abbey business or at court, and the monks could take refuge in troubled times. Many of these houses are still standing. The Maison d'Ourscamp now houses the Association for the Safeguard of Historic Paris, in the Marais quarter.

Further Reading

Various authors, *Bernard de Clairvaux, Une Eglise Aimée*, Strasbourg, 1990
Various authors, *Studi su San Bernardo di Chiaravalle nell'Ottavo Centenario della Canonizzazione* Frosinone, 1975
BADSTÜBNER, E. *Kirchen der Mönche*, Leipzig, 1984
BEDINI, B. *Le Abazie Cistercensi d'Italia*, Casamari, 1980
BILLINGS, M. *The Cross and The Crescent*, London, 1987
BORDONOVE, G. *Les Templiers*, Paris, 1977

BOUTON, J. *Histoire de l'Ordre de Cîteaux*, Westmalle, 1959

BRAUNFELS, W. *Monasteries of Western Europe*, London, 1972

BROOKE, C. *Monasteries of the World*, Ware, 1974

BUTLER, L. and GIVEN-WILSON, C. *Medieval Monasteries of Great Britain*, London, 1979

COCHERIL, M. *Dictionnaire des Monastères Cisterciens*, Rochefort, 1976

DIMIER, A. *L'Art Cistercien*, Vols I and II, La-Pierre-Qui-Vire, 1971/72

DUBY, G. *Saint Bernard et l'Art Cistercien*, Paris, 1979

DE LA FOYE, J. *Ondes de Vie, Ondes de Mort*, Paris, 1975

FERGUSSON, P. *Architecture of Solitude*, Princeton, 1984

FRACCARO DE LONGHI, L. *L'Architettura delle Chiese Cistercensi Italiane*, Milan, 1958

DE GASTYNE, T. *Vie Quotidienne d'un Moine à Fontenay au XIIIe Siècle*, Montbard, 1987

GERVERS, M. (ed.) *The Second Crusade and the Cistercians*, New York, 1992

HALLAM, E. and others, *The Plantagenet Chronicles*, London, 1986

HASKINS, C. *The Renaissance of the 12th Century*, Harvard, 1927

JANAUSCHEK, L. *Originum Cisterciensium*, Vienna 1877, repr. Ridgewood 1964

KING, E. *Medieval England*, Oxford, 1988

LEFEVRE, R. and others, *Tra le Abbazie del Lazio*, Rome, 1987

LEFF, G. *Medieval Thought*, London, 1958

LEKAI, L. J. *The Cistercians: Ideals and Reality*, Kalamazoo, 1977

MAZZUCCO, G. *Monasteri Benedettini nella Laguna Veneta*, Venice, 1983

VAN DER MEER, F. *Atlas de l'Ordre Cistercien*, Paris, Bruxelles, 1965

MONTAGU OF BEAULIEU and TOMKINS, S. *Beaulieu Palace House and Abbey*, Beaulieu, 1988

NEGRI, D. *Abbazie Cistercensi in Italia*, Pistoia, 1981

NEW, A. *A Guide to the Abbeys of England and Wales*, London, 1985

NORTON, C. and PARK, D. (ed.) *Cistercian Art And Architecture in the British Isles*, Cambridge, 1985

OURSEL, R. *L'Esprit de Cîteaux*, La-Pierre-Qui-Vire, 1978

PRAWER, J. *The World of the Crusaders*, London, 1972

PRESSOUYRE, L. *Le Rêve Cistercien*, Paris, 1990

PRESSOUYRE, L. (ed.) *L'Espace Cistercien*, Paris, 1994

PRESSOUYRE, L. and KINDER, T. (ed.) *St Bernard & Le Monde Cistercien*, Paris, 1992

RILEY-SMITH, L. and J. *The Crusades*, London, 1981

RUNCIMAN, S. *A History of the Crusades*, Cambridge, 1952

SCHNEIDER, A. *Die Cistercienser, Geschichte, Geist, Kunst*, Cologne, 1974

STALLEY, R. *The Cistercian Monasteries of Ireland*, Yale, 1987

SYDOW, J., MIKKERS, E. and HERTKORN, A. *Die Zisterzienser*, Stuttgart, 1991

VINCENOT, H. *Les Etoiles de Compostelle*, Paris, 1982

WILLEMS, E. *Esquisse Historique de l'Ordre de Cîteaux*, Liège, 1957

Index